DORDT INFORMATION SERVICE

3 6520 0040231 Q

D0328881

Springer Series on Social Work

Albert R. Roberts, D.S.W., Series Editor

Advisory Board: Joseph D. Anderson, D.S.W., Barbara Berkman, D.S.W., Paul H. Ephross, Ph.D., Sheldon R. Gelman, Ph.D., Nancy A. Humphreys, D.S.W., Louise P. Shoemaker, D.S.W., and Julia Watkins, Ph.D.

Volume 1
Battered Women and their Families
Intervention Strategies and Treatment Programs
Albert R. Roberts, D.S.W.

Volume 2
Disability, Work, and Social Policy
Models for Social Welfare
Aliki Coudroglou, D.S.W. and Dennis L. Poole, Ph.D.

Volume 3
Social Policy and the Rural Setting
Julia M. Watkins, Ph.D. and Dennis A. Watkins, Ph.D.

Volume 4
Clinical Social Work in Health Settings
A Guide to Professional Practice with Exemplars
Thomas Owen Carlton, D.S.W.

Volume 5
Social Work in the Emergency Room
Carole W. Soskis, M.S.W., J.D.

Volume 6
Task-Centered Practice with Families and Groups
Anne E. Fortune, Ph.D.

Volume 7
Widow-to-Widow
Phyllis R. Silverman, Ph.D.

Phyllis R. Silverman, Ph.D., is a Professor in the Social Work and Health Program of the Massachusetts General Hospital Institute of Health Professions. She also holds an appointment in the Department of Psychiatry at Harvard Medical School, where she developed the concept of the Widow-to-Widow program and directed the research project that demonstrated its effectiveness. She has served as consultant to several task forces on bereavement and primary prevention convened by the National Institute of Mental Health; has consulted with agencies across the country on issues of bereavement, mutual help, and prevention; and has worked in community agencies both as a case worker and as a researcher. In addition to her social work degree from the Smith College School of Social Work, she holds an M.S. in Hygiene from the Harvard School of Public Health and a Ph.D. from the Florence Heller School for Advanced Studies in Social Welfare at Brandeis University. Her publications include *Helping Each Other in Widowhood, If You Will Lift the Load I Will Lift It Too, Mutual Help Groups: A Guide for Mental Health Professionals, Mutual Help Groups: Organization and Development,* and *Helping Women Cope with Grief.*

Widow-to-Widow

Phyllis R. Silverman, Ph.D.

Springer Publishing Company
New York

Copyright © 1986 by Springer Publishing Company, Inc.

All rights reserved

No part of this publication may be reproduced, stored in a retrieval system, or transmitted in any form or by any means, electronic, mechanical, photocopying, recording, or otherwise, without the prior permission of Springer Publishing Company, Inc.

Springer Publishing Company, Inc.
536 Broadway
New York, New York 10012

86 87 88 89 90 / 5 4 3 2 1

Library of Congress Cataloging-in-Publication Data

Silverman, Phyllis R.
  Widow-to-widow.

  Bibliography
  Includes index.
  1. Widows—United States.   2. Widows—United States—Psychology.
3. Bereavement.   4. Self-help groups—United States.   I. Title.
HQ1058.5.U5S57   1986   305.4'89'0654   85-22108
ISBN 0-8261-5030-6

Printed in the United States of America

Contents

Preface

You need to talk with someone else who is a widow—who really knows what it is like. I thought I was the only one in the world who felt this lonely and was so afraid. [40-year-old woman, widowed one year]

Widowhood affects about three out of four women. This is a book about women as widows and about widows helping other widows. The various chapters bring together current research on bereavement, on the psychology of women, on the problems of the widow, and on the effects of mutual-help interventions. For the first time, the findings of the original Widow-to-Widow project are presented in their entirety between the covers of one book.

In the Widow-to-Widow project carried out at Harvard Medical School from 1967 to 1973, women who had been widowed for some time reached out to every newly widowed woman in a target community. They offered friendship, support, and information on how to cope. This was an unsolicited offer of assistance, so that the new widow did not need to decide if she needed help and what type of help she needed.

This project has served as the basis for a growing number of mutual-help programs for widows throughout the United States and in several other countries. By integrating the Widow-to-Widow findings with several other bodies of knowledge, I hope to create a new appreciation of the way women live their lives, how widows change to accommodate to their loss, and how mutual help can facilitate this process.

The book focuses not only on widows' feelings of grief but also on how widowhood changes women's lives. "Widow" is a social role that signifies change in a woman's place in society and that also forces her to change her sense of self. While a woman is defined socially and legally as a widow from the minute her husband dies, she will need time, perhaps years, to understand what she has lost, to recognize that her old definition of herself may no longer be relevant to her current world, and to build a new sense of self. Her grief is therefore not an illness from which she will "recover" and for which she can be treated. Bereavement initiates a process of change in which the widow cannot be cured of grief but is changed by it. In one way or another, she has to relinquish the role of wife, to accept the role of widow, and ultimately to redefine herself as a woman.

Bereavement marks the beginning of a psychosocial transition entailing several stages of change toward accommodation in new social roles. Since many aspects of a woman's psychological development are reflected in her experience during this period, widows have much to teach us about women's social adaptation and identity formation. The literature on the psychology of women that has appeared in the past decade focuses on the special meaning of relationships and their role in the way women experience themselves and develop a sense of identity. This work recognizes and values the positive aspects of women's involvements with others and the ways they live their lives. While men also need others, their self-development focuses more on individuation and autonomy. A woman's identity is largely framed by her relationships and is attached to the roles associated with these relationships. In losing an essential relationship, she loses an essential part of herself. Her grief is pervasive: she confronts losses and the challenge of change in herself, in her relationships, and in her social position.

This view of a widow as a woman in transition supports a different approach to helping in which we focus on the widow's need to change roles and develop a new position in society. My research and the subsequent work of others has pointed to the special value of peers in helping to make such changes. This approach departs from more traditional views of widowhood and the customary medical-model interventions that suggest "treatment," with the goals of "healing" and "recovery" for the mourner. This approach uses mutual help, with the goal of facilitating change. Helpers are widows who have coped successfully with a similar transition, and the help they offer is based on their own experience. The findings of the Widow-to-Widow project show what women can do for themselves and each other in order to emerge from the experience changed, but not "cured."

The book is divided into four sections. The first presents a view of bereavement as a transition, with a perspective on the needs of women and the effectiveness of mutual-help efforts at times of transition. The next two sections report on the history, organization, and findings of the Widow-to-Widow project. The last section shows how the program helped women move through the transition from wife to widow to woman.

Acknowledgments

There are many people I want to thank for their help in making this book possible. Gerald Caplan is foremost in my mind, for his excellence as a teacher who introduced me to concepts of prevention in mental health when I was his student at the Harvard School of Public Health, and for his willingness to support me in trying new ideas when I came to work for him at the Department of Psychiatry at Harvard Medical School. In addition, without the cooperation and the financial support of the National Funeral Directors Association and the Massachusetts Funeral Directors Association, the Widow-to-Widow program would have remained only an idea. Howard Raether, Executive Director of the NFDA, and Sheldon Daly, Executive Director of the MFDA at that time, were instrumental in recruiting the cooperation of these organizations. I am particularly grateful to Carolyn Mercer McFadden, who edited this book for me. It is a result of her skill as a colleague and friend that this book is both readable and coherent. She was there for moral support and to help me clarify my thinking. I also want to thank Sandra Sumner who, with careful attention to detail, typed this manuscript and who was able to smile with me while trying to meet my unrealistic deadlines.

The demonstration project would never have moved from the planning table to implementation without the wonderful women who came to work with me. Adele Cooperband, the late Dorothy McKenzie, Mary Pettipas, Elizabeth Wilson, and Cary Wynn were the aides who reached out to the newly widowed.

The success of the program was a result of their willingness to share the pain of their own widowhood and their mistakes and successes with the women they served. All the widows who have come afterwards, who both received and gave help in programs modeled after the original Widow-to-Widow program, owe these women a debt of gratitude for all that they gave to make this experiment work. I would also like to thank Ruby Abraham and Cecile Strugnell, my research associates, who facilitated the documentation of what we did. Ruby Abraham, in addition, was responsible for all the research associated with the Widowed Service Line. I am also grateful to Ruth Abrams and Faye Snyder, who managed the project after Gila and Aaron were born.

Finally, I want to say thank you to my family. Without them I would have been finished in a quarter of the time, but without them this would not have been as rich a book. To my husband Sam and to our children, Ann, Bill, Nancy, Gila, and Aaron, who grew up with this project learning that there is life and there is death—thank you.

I

Theoretical Perspectives on Grief and Helping

1   Grief as a Transition

Bereavement is a specific state initiated by the death of someone who is close and dear. Bereavement usually brings on grieving, an expression of feelings through crying, pining, general
malaise, and psychological, or even physical pain. This chapter
explores the nature of the grieving process, how it unfolds, and
how it may be resolved. As with the book as a whole, this
discussion focuses particularly on the special challenges that
widows confront when their husbands die.

The Expression of Grief

Bereaved people do not behave in a fashion that is typical for
them. Responding to an extreme situation, they are experiencing
extreme feelings, and they act uncharacteristically. While some
of these atypical responses will be idiosyncratic to a bereaved
individual, certain patterns in the expression of grief are found
in most mourners. Lazare (1979) has described these well. Drawing on the descriptions by Lindemann (1944), Parkes (1972),
Maddison and Raphael (1977), Marris (1958), and Kübler-Ross
(1969), Lazare summarized what is known about their reactions
as follows:

> The first response to learning of the loss is shock and disbelief,
> "Impossible: you are joking." "I don't believe it." Immediately
> thereafter there may be outbursts of tearfulness and restlessness

alternating with numbness, blunted affect, or frozen withdrawal. This period may last from a few hours to a few weeks. With the full realization of loss, the bereaved, as described by Lindemann, experiences a syndrome of somatic distress, characterized by feelings of tightness in the throat, choking with shortness of breath, the need for sighing, an empty feeling in the abdomen, lack of muscular power, and intense tension or mental pain. This somatic distress, precipitated by mention of the deceased, occurs in waves lasting from 20 minutes to 1 hour. The bereaved becomes intensely preoccupied with the deceased. "I am completely occupied by him." "I am so full of him." "I wish that I could get my mind off him." At the same time the bereaved may take on symptoms, mannerisms, habits or personality traits of the deceased. "Sometimes when I am speaking, I do not know whether it is he or me." He yearns and pines for the deceased, walks about restlessly, as if searching for him, sees people whom, for an instant, he mistakes for the deceased, and sometimes calls out his name. He may express irritability, anger, bitterness, resentment, and rage over the loss. These feelings may be directed toward the deceased or toward the family and friends in close proximity. There is often an attempt to focus blame and responsibility, particularly on himself. "How could this have happened?" "Why didn't I insist that he see the doctor?" "I should have known." "I should not have let him drive by himself."

The preoccupation with the deceased and the psychological and somatic distress is so great that the bereaved is unable to concentrate or maintain the usual patterns of behavior. There is no zest. Every task seems a major effort. Time drags. Life seems to have no meaning.

As the grief process continues, the bereaved reviews a variety of memories associated with the deceased and his relationship to him. He discusses these memories in considerable detail and, stimulated by the repeated inquiries of visitors, he reviews them, again and again. Eventually, he regains interest in the outside world and is able to reinvest in new relationships. [p. 498]

Grief ends, in this view, when the bereaved person has finally let go of the investment in the deceased. The person does not actually forget the deceased, but changes the relationship so that he or she can invest in new relationships. While it is correct that the bereaved person must change the relationship to the de-

HQ 1073. V34 1982
Personal Guide
Vail, Elaine

HQ 1058.5. US S57
Widow 2 Widow 1986
Silverman

BF 789. D4 S36 1978
Psychology of
Schulz

...nship does not necessarily mean ...hat affects the rest of the bereaved ...ert Anderson described his feelings ...is first wife: "I have a new life. . . . ...oes not end a relationship, which ...r's mind toward some resolution ... p. 77).

...ught pictures grief as having an end, ...ontrast, bereaved people who have ...iences have reported that it took at ...y could begin to look to the future ...75). Mental health professionals, in-...rge L. Engel's paper (1961), which reinforces their predisposition to think in this way, see bereavement as an acute illness. They talk about "recovering" from grief and set a time limit for when the bereaved person should finish mourning. Beyond this time limit, they see the grief as symptomatic of psychopathology. As the continued mourning becomes for them a symptom of psychological disturbance, they prescribe professional treatment. Two fundamental questions must be addressed: Is grief indeed an illness? Is recovery possible?

Grief as an Illness

Engel, in 1961, and others since (e.g., Parkes, 1972) have described mourners' reactions to their losses as symptoms of psychiatric disorder or disease. Engel argued that grief shares with disease the features of intense suffering, a consistent etiologic factor, a temporary impairment of capacity to function, a discrete syndrome with a common symptomatology, and a predictable course. In support of this approach, Parkes wrote, "I know of only one functional psychiatric disorder whose cause is known, whose features are distinctive and whose course is usually predictable, and that is grief, the reaction to loss" (1972, p. 6). Parkes makes an analogy between a wound and grief. The natural, uncomplicated physical reaction to a wound is self-limited, adaptive, and reparative; and it represents a healthy reaction to a common life stress. A complicated reaction would entail imperfect healing, perhaps with a persistent infection or an unsightly scar. Similarly, the reaction to grief is conceived of as uncomplicated (self-limited, adaptive, and so forth) or complicated (not healing, scarring, and so forth).

When bereavement is understood to be an illness, the words used to describe the resolution of grief are "healing" and "recovery." If intervention or any help is needed, the mourner is encouraged to seek "treatment" that will effect a "cure." Such a framework basically characterizes grief as a foreign force that has invaded the bereaved person's body. It removes grief from the realm of universal human experience and places it in the domain of the alien. Grief is therefore something which, with proper assistance, one could and should minimize or avoid. Also implicit in this approach are the notions that (1) a spontaneous healing process will occur if the mourner has sufficient psychological health, (2) the mourner should grieve in a particular way, and (3) the mourner should seek a professional person's privileged knowledge about how to grieve. In the words of one widow, "The doctor said I would feel better in time. I would get over it. When that didn't happen I was sure something was wrong with me."

The illness framework implies recovery. Help therefore focuses on assisting the bereaved person to give up the loved one, in the language of psychoanalysis to "decathect the deceased." Recovery implies a return to prior functioning. When a wound heals, the wounded person usually seeks a return to prior activities and levels of functioning. With grief and bereavement, this may not be possible, or even desirable. Freud himself, in a letter to a friend whose son had died, wrote,

> There is no restitutum ad integrum after a serious affective loss. The structure of one's inner world . . . will never be the same. Not only is the identity of self changed, but also that of the outer world is different. . . . We know that the most poignant grief is blunted after such a loss; but we remain inconsolable and never can find a substitute. Whoever takes his place, even if he were to fill it completely will always remain totally different, and actually that is as it should be. It is the only way to preserve a love that in reality one did not wish to relinquish. [Von Witzleben, 1958]

Since grief is unending, recovery is not possible. With time, grief becomes intense and takes new forms. These new expressions offer the mourner new perspectives on the bereavement experience, but they are still expressions of grief. Rather than looking for the mourner's recovery, it may be more appropriate to look for accommodation and change.

To seek a cure for one's responses to an irretrievable and real loss—the end of life for a person one has loved and still loves—seems inconsistent with the nature of the event. Whether the cure is called decathecting or letting go, it would seem to deny the meaning that the deceased person has had in one's inner and outer life. Can a mother or father whose child has died ever return to life as it was before the death? Their lives included, indeed revolved about, that child; with the child's death, life is inexorably changed. If the child was their only child, then they have also lost their roles as parents. Pincus (1975) identified a psychologically healthy process that she called incorporation and in which "the lost person is internalized and becomes part of the bereaved" (p. 124). Marris (1974) described a second type of process, wherein the bereaved person finds continuity between past and present by detaching the familiar meanings of life from the relationship and reestablishing them independently. He suggested that a person masters grief not by ceasing to care about the dead person, but by abstracting what was fundamentally important in the relationship and rehabilitating it. He called this a process of reformulation rather than substitution. People don't give up the past, they change their relationship to it, and this takes place over an extended period of time. Bereavement can best be seen not as an illness but as a period of transition.

The Nature of Transition

Inherent in the concept of transition is the idea that a change is taking place. Change implies a need for modification, transformation, or alteration. James Tyhurst (1958), a pioneer in the study of transition states, observed that not only should the focus be on the change itself but also on the state of the change, the process of going from one situation to another. He was therefore concerned with the social and psychological circumstances that enable the process of change. This suggests that any intervention offered to someone in transition should aim to enhance the person's competency in traversing the period of change.

Change takes place over time, and the time of change can be divided into stages. At each stage, the individual has different needs and different tasks to accomplish. Moving from one stage to the next generally requires having completed some of the work of the preceding stage. The ultimate result is an accommodation, rather than a return to an earlier level of functioning. Since the work of transition is to move from one stage to the next, any help must facilitate this movement, and the help must therefore be responsive to the individual's point in the transition, as well as to the individual's need for support between stages. Ideally, many kinds of help would be available as responses to the variety of needs and tasks associated with each stage.

Following Tyhurst's thinking, a transition has three critical characteristics: (1) there is a disequilibrating event or series of events, (2) a role change is involved, and (3) change takes place over time.

Disequilibrating Events

An event or a series of events that have a disruptive effect on those involved, thus causing stress, are disequilibrating. Stress develops because a person no longer can function as before. While the onset of the disequilibrium can be gradual or sudden, anticipated or unanticipated, change is always involved, and stress is typically and unavoidably associated with change. Disequilibrating events take varied forms, ranging from the birth of a baby to the death of a parent. The challenge is not how to avoid the stress, which is inevitable, but to recognize that it is appropriate and to learn what might moderate or manage it. Individuals' responses vary according to their preparation for managing change. Their preparation in turn depends on a number of individual variables: experience with change, personal flexibility in accepting the need for change, and knowledge about the nature of the current transition. Also crucial in individuals' preparation are the attitudes, values, and rituals in the larger social network, since these will affect how the individuals perceive and react to their situation, and the meaning that the situation has for their lives.

A person's past experience shapes his or her view of the life cycle and can be a source of perspective for approaching a new situation. If an individual has experienced a change and managed it successfully, he or she theoretically would find a new situation requiring change to be less threatening. Every adult has experienced many transitions over the formative years of childhood and has had at least some degree of success in having arrived at adulthood. Often, however, people are not fully aware of their own process of change and do not generalize from one period to another.

Ideally, individuals would develop a schema or schemata that incorporated an evolving sense of self and a repertoire of responses when change is required. This repertoire would include a vocabulary for describing and understanding change in general, as well as the particular change associated with the imminent transition. It also would include an ideology that gave meaning to the event. Ideologies and language can be integrative. They define an event as manageable or overwhelming. They mediate the stress associated with it. They determine what degree of change may be required. For example, a transition can be defined as a problem or as an expected occurrence. Grief, if defined as a problem of illness, is a condition for which treatment and cure are sought in order to remove or limit the stress. Defined as a natural reaction to death, an inevitable human experience with which everyone must cope, grief would be expected to bring stress and pain, which in turn would be seen as legitimate and appropriate. Socially established rituals would facilitate mourning and offer ways of coping with the stress.

Ideology and language are transmitted in part by the larger culture. The sense of self and the repertoire of responses that individuals develop are embedded in the values and attitudes current in the larger society. If that society focuses on maintaining a closed system with fixed parameters, then its members will have a less difficult time learning to cope with a transition. Rules, customs, and rituals would govern behavior at such times and would direct the process of change in an acceptable context.

In a more open system, such well-equipped ideologies are less likely, and people have less guidance. Contemporary Western society admits few rituals for helping people to cope. In the case of bereavement, for example, the funeral is currently criticized as too costly. While we largely ignore its ritual functions, it is the last public act honoring the deceased and is a forum for mourners to acknowledge their loss and express their grief. The success of Sheehy's *Passages* (1976) reflects a current search for ways of viewing and reacting to change over the life cycle.

Adaptation involves learning, and the adaptive strategies people develop are affected by their opportunities for learning. To be effective, these learning opportunities need to supply pertinent information. Given the proper tools, most people are capable of dealing with any transition state.

Role Changes

Transitions generally involve status changes for the affected individuals, meaning that they must redefine the roles they perform within their social networks. Letting go of familiar roles is not simple. Peter Marris (1974) noted that every change entails a loss, if not actually a death, and the need to give up an old, inapplicable role. He observed people's reluctance to give up the past and the familiar, and he labeled this wish for things to remain the same as the "conservative impulse." The individual does let go, however, by integrating some aspect of the past into the new role or changed situation.

This integration resembles a cognitive process identified by Piaget (1965). Children who tried to apply formerly workable strategies to new situations learned that they could not assimilate certain aspects of the past into the present because these aspects were no longer applicable. Eventually the children accommodated by developing a new schema for dealing with the new situation. Within this new schema were remnants of the prior schemas.

The same cognitive process applies to adult learning. In responding to a death, the mourner should not be expected to give up the past but instead to find ways to incorporate aspects of past relationships into the present and future. Symbols that convey immortality for the dead person supply a means of remembering and also a bridge to the future. If, as noted, people let go when some of the past can be assimilated into the present, then incorporating elements of the past into new roles and schemata will help to bridge the gap between past and future.

A colleague and I (Silverman & Silverman, 1979) have distinguished two modes of coping: denial and negation. Denial may be part of the initial reaction to the death and is normal during the first months of bereavement. Denial can be expressed in many ways, including silence. It can be a temporary attempt to wipe out the past or a method of acting as if nothing has happened, as if no death has occurred and, indirectly, as if no life has been lived. Denial in the widow is manifest in her inability to think of herself as widowed. Denial generally is mediated with time; as a woman finds it impossible to avoid the reality, she has to change the daily habits of living that involved the deceased.

Negation, which follows denial, gives significance to the death by providing for a new and continuing life and is a way of actively resolving the dilemma. Negation can be expressed in many ways: in rituals that honor the memory of the deceased, in memorials provided by descendants, and in acts that the deceased person would have approved. As Lifton (1974) suggests, these expressions give symbolic immortality to the deceased.

When a death occurs, the living must be psychologically committed to moving from the old conditions to the new. Lopata (1973) has offered another perspective on factors that make this particular role change so difficult. She observed that the less well regarded and well defined the new social role is, the more difficult the shift will be. The role of wife for most women traditionally has been honorable and desirable. But the role of widow occupies a marginal social position. The ease with which an individual accepts the need to learn a new role is inversely related to the intensity of the stigma associated with the new role. Difficulty in changing roles may also relate to how much the old role has framed an individual's identity. Altering or giving up an old role will be especially difficult if the person derived much of her or his sense of self from it. Thus, as people change roles they need to feel legitimated as individuals in their new roles and, at the same time, may need to cope with the stigma attached to the new role.

Change over Time

Adaptation to any change, including a transition state, takes place over time. Widowed people are dismayed when their relatives become impatient with them for continuing to grieve and are themselves unprepared for the long time it takes to accommodate. Like their relatives, they expected and hoped that mourning would end in a matter of weeks. In societies with established rites of passage, the time periods for mourning are well marked, with established rituals for helping people to cope.

To a certain extent, every transition has a beginning and an end; in between them, the individual does the work of the transition. Most people do not know what this work involves. The work of transition can be divided into phases, each with its own tasks associated with it. Tyhurst (1958) and Bowlby (1961) have described three stages of transitions associated with loss: impact, recoil, and accommodation. (While other theorists have talked about four or five stages, three will suffice for this discussion.)

Impact. The impact stage starts when a critical event occurs, such as when a child is born, at the moment of death, or when a critical diagnosis is made. The primary emotional response to impact is numbness. The person does not grasp, even disbelieves, the reality of what has happened, reflecting a very strong reluctance to relinquish the past. Behavior appropriate to the past role still dominates. Old role definitions and relationships still guide behavior and frame the person's self-image.

The function of the numbing (or denial as it is sometimes called) is to allow the individual to act, for example, allowing a life-saving but frightening operation, or enabling the person to plan the funeral without being overwhelmed by the full meaning of what has happened. At this stage, a person thinks, "This can't be happening to me. I'll wake up and find it is a dream." Denial is not necessarily something to be avoided. It enables a person to take in reality a little at a time until the person is ready to recognize what is really happening. In transitions beginning with happy events, or transitions of incorporation, the numbness takes on the quality of incredulousness that such a good and wonderful event has occurred, and a person thinks, "This has happened to *me*?"

Recoil.   The second stage, recoil, is characterized by a growing recognition of the reality of the change. The numbness has lifted, and in a sense "the honeymoon is over." People at this point are more able to allow their feelings to come out. In a transition of separation, the recoil stage is the time for the emergence of all the despair, all the loneliness, and all the pain associated with the loss. These feelings come up as frustration and tension mount over the inability to continue living as if nothing happened. As the person realizes that living by the old rules is no longer possible, a crisis in meaning develops. Stress arises in response to the vacuum that exists when new rules have not yet replaced the old, inapplicable ones. At this point, people know that they cannot go back, but they are still not ready to go forward.

Accommodation.   Accommodation is under way when the individual has found a new direction and has begun to assume a new identity. The goal of the accommodation stage is not acceptance. Acceptance is only a part of accommodation. Avery Weissman (1977) noted that people who did not quietly accept their imminent deaths from cancer, but who strove to maintain involvement in living and hopes for the future, had a higher survival rate. There can be no single script for accommodation. An individual must find a way to live in a changed situation.

Accommodation can mean dramatic growth, or quiet reorientation, depending upon the individual, the nature of the transition, and the way the work of transition proceeds.

Grief as a Transition

We must all live with the fact that death occurs and that to be bereft is part of the human condition. Grief is a process rather than a state, and while its onset may be clear, its ending is not. Grief entails coping with social as well as emotional losses; it requires a person to change and to accommodate. The way people react to bereavement depends partly on their knowledge of death and grieving and partly on their individual styles of coping. All men and women need to learn to accept death, to cope with bereavement, and above all to help themselves through the process of grieving and accommodation. Research has concluded that the acceptance of death is learned; that is, people accept death when they learn to cope with it. It has been found that most mature people had not learned to accept and cope with death. My own work with the widowed has produced parallel findings: Just as people must learn to be parents, they need to learn to be widows or widowers. Rather than an illness-to-health model, we need an educational model of bereavement and grief that considers the conditions that maximize learning and the person's ability to use new information.

The concept of transition elaborated on earlier supports such a model. Applied to the widow's bereavement and grieving, the disequilibrating event is the husband's death. Change takes place, including the process of grieving, over time. And the transition involves a critical role change, from the role of wife to the role of widow and on to other roles. An educational model tailored to this transition would facilitate change over time, so that the widow would achieve new perspectives on feelings and behavior and gradually assume new roles and new ways of relating to herself and the world around her.

While sociologists, such as Lopata (1973), have understood the bereavement process in terms of transition, most psychological theories of bereavement do not consider the need to give up an old identity and to build a new one. Parkes (1972) wrote of his concern for widows who seemed to have resolved their acute grief but still felt dissatisfied. From the sociological perspective, Parkes probably was observing the widows' dissatisfaction over the loss of the wife role and their need to build new roles, which they had not yet done.

The Onset of Transition

A personal transition begins with a disequilibrating event, requires a role change, and entails a period of time for coping with the disequilibrating experience and for making the role change.

A husband can die at any time. How upsetting his death will be to his widow depends on a variety of factors, including his (and her) age and how she views his death. Certainly, the death of a young husband, unexpected and out of turn in the life cycle, will tax whatever meaning the young widow's philosophical or religious orientation attaches to death in general. A young woman, recognizing the reality of death perhaps for the first time, may be particularly shattered by it happening to her peer. Younger people may have no ready framework in which to put such an experience. Still, an older woman may be no more prepared for her husband's death.

Social Attitudes toward Grief and Widows

In our society, lack of preparation is not associated with age. It reflects a general attitude in which we do not want to face the meaning of death in life. This attitude is not so much a denial or an avoidance of death itself, as is sometimes thought. It is a lack of knowledge about how to accept the fact that people die and integrate it into a view of the life that goes on. It is the pain associated with grief that the society wants to deny and avoid.

In this context, aside from the initial comfort she may receive, a widow of any age will feel isolated and alone in her struggle. She also actually may feel rejected, an untouchable in a world she once knew as safe. She is confused and puzzled by the reactions of her friends and family. In the words of one young widow, "Being a widow is like having a contagious disease." People pull back, some with more forthrightness than others: "I can't come to visit you in your house; you remind me that I lost my best friend and I can't face that."

The problem seems to stem from the inability of most people, including professionally trained people, to accept death as an inevitable part of the life cycle. Death is seen as an affront, a failure that should not have occurred. One newly widowed woman recalled the doctor's reaction to her husband's death:

> He had a heart condition. If the doctor knew that people rarely recover from this type of attack he did not say so. We really believed that he would be cured. We had such faith in what the doctor could do. Then, when he died, the doctor kept saying he was sorry—sort of saying it should not have happened. I would have laughed if I hadn't been so upset. I ended up reassuring the doctor.

Ironically, as Robert J. Lifton (1979) has reminded us, "These days, in fact, one has the impression, at least in America, that death has been all too much found" (p. 4). The number of seminars and courses presented on death are proliferating, and there is an enormous literature designed to help people face and talk about death. In contrast, Lifton points out, "Much more elusive is the psychological relationship between death and the flow of life" (p. 4). People fail to integrate into their lives the fact that we are all mortal, not by avoiding death itself, but by avoiding grief. From an early age, we know that physical death takes place, but this knowledge only becomes real when we experience the psychological impact of a bereaved person expressing their feelings. Thus, we ask the bereaved to be circumspect, to contain their feelings, to act almost as if nothing had happened. Professionals focus on recovery—and look for it within six months. As the following two quotes from widows show, friends and relatives reinforce the widow's attempts at self-control:

For months everyone kept praising me about how well I was doing. I was calm and controlled. I did not know that I had that much control. They never knew what I was really feeling inside, and to this day I am sure they were grateful that I didn't tell them how upset I was. I really felt like screaming, "This isn't happening to me."

My family doesn't want to see me upset. I've even noticed neighbors avoid me in the supermarket. I try not to cry or show my sadness, I keep wondering why I feel this way when everyone says I should be over it. After all, he's been dead six months. I kept wondering what I was doing wrong, what was wrong with me that I was not doing better.

The widow takes on the role of victim, blaming herself. At a time when she should feel cared about and supported, she feels isolated and defective. She finds that her grief is not admissible, that her community has no room for mourners. In all the current talk about death and how to help people die, few have spoken about the long pain that goes on beyond the funeral and the initial period of mourning. The extreme feelings associated with expressions of grief are regarded as embarrassing. Not surprisingly, few rituals exist to help people mourn and to guide others in their reactions to the mourning. Without such rituals or customs, and finding her grief unacceptable, the widow is stigmatized. She tends to blame herself, fixing fault within herself and not in the reactions of others. Her equilibrium is upset, as she receives no support for what she thought would be expected of her—pain and sorrow.

The Lack of Ritual

Over the past century, ritual mourning practices have fallen into disuse in Western societies, as we have rationalized away the meaning of death in life and have generally abandoned sacred rituals. Rituals can help to focus attention on the meaning of the loss, can serve to legitimate feelings, and can offer ways of coping by furnishing new behavior patterns as alternatives to the person's habitual daily routines of interaction with the deceased. In short, rituals can make life easier for the bereaved.

As Gorer (1965) has noted, the demise of sacred ritual around death has left a void in contemporary society. No rituals of transition have developed to replace the sacred customs that have been set aside as being no longer relevant. Today's trend is to dispose quickly of the body and get right back to things as usual, depriving the mourner of an opportunity to grieve and to have more than token consolation from friends and family. This modern trend is also somewhat disrespectful to the deceased: People are often encouraged to act as if the dead person had never existed.

While we generally still do have some ritual of burial that marks the death, in some traditions and in other societies rituals pay attention to the longer term. Traditional Jewish mourning ritual includes public honoring of the dead, consoling of the mourners, bringing the whole family together to share their grief, and then, over a year, a series of events and gatherings in which the mourner can express his or her loss and can accommodate gradually.

Van Gennup (1960) describes a several-stage process of mourning that he calls rites of passage marking the separation of the living and the dead. First is the burial of the dead, then visualizing of the dead person at rest in the land of the deceased from which there is no return, and then a severing of ties with the deceased, or a cessation of the role obligations that have kept the involvement alive. In some societies, death and the rituals following it do not end the obligation, but only change it. For example, in ancient China, one's obligations to one's ancestors continued forever. In many societies, the rituals of mourning make for a sharp distinction between the duties of the individual who is a mourner and the duties the person would address had there been no death. Daily life routines are interrupted, and behavior changes are legitimated. Later will come the rituals of reentry or reintegration. Participating in rituals such as these, the bereaved person simultaneously expresses the different conditions she or he is experiencing and shows solidarity with the social group of which she or he is a part.

The widow in our society suffers not only from the pain associated with her loss, but also from the lack of rituals that guide her mourning, help her understand what is happening, facilitate the comfort offered by others, and help her reorganize her life in light of the many changes caused by her husband's death. These changes are largely associated with the loss of her role as wife and the need to find a new role.

2 Meanings of the Transition from Wife to Widow

The Wife Role and Woman's Identity

A *role* is a socially prescribed pattern of behavior corresponding to an individual's status in a particular society. In her married status, a woman is assigned the role of wife; in this role, she performs certain obligations to her mate and she also receives a legal and social position relative to other members of the society. Since the role of wife involves both a relationship to a mate and a status in relation to the rest of society, it provides a social and legal frame for a woman's identity.

Although the same is true socially and legally for a man in the role of husband, it differs psychologically. The spousal role is more central to the woman's sense of identity, to her experience of herself as a person. This is so because historically the roles of husband and wife were endowed with different intrinsic meanings. Upon marrying, the woman became her husband's property. She was a fragile object and needed to be sheltered by her husband. For her putative benefit, she was forced by law to defer to her husband's will.

Vestiges of this view of woman as dependent child can still be seen in our legal system (Freeman, 1973). Although the Equal Rights Amendment (ERA) has been passed in 25 states, although a woman today cannot be denied credit in her own

name, and although her standing, regardless of her marital status, is legally the same as a man's, practical realities reflect more
ancient values. The ERA has not passed in the country as a
whole, and the legal standing of women varies from state to
state. Women are often still seen as acting only with their husbands' permission, as reflected in this quote from a letter my
husband received after I had returned from a lecture tour in
1975: "I want to thank you for allowing your wife to come to our
state and address our group about the work she is doing."
Current political and theoretical efforts focus on changing both
the legal status of women and the social and psychological
perceptions of women (Friedan, 1964, 1976; Miller, 1976). Yet
these are the efforts of a small minority, and the lag continues
between ideology and practice.

　　Children are always raised so that their self-images will
coincide with prevailing views of their future roles. Until recently, from girl to woman, the female child was taught to fill
subordinate positions—fragile child, devoted mother, or husband's companion (Rothman, 1978). Above all, her social learning was that as an adult she would assume the role of wife,
which also would give her an adult identity. Most of the literature published during this century on the psychology of women
supports the view of women as passive, as looking to their mates
for their sense of identity and their place in the world. In 1945
Helene Deutsch offered the still-dominant framework for understanding female psychology. She established the view that
women are psychologically passive and dependent, while men
are active and autonomously assertive.

　　Not long ago, any woman who was assertive was considered neurotic. A healthy woman would not set active goals in
pursuit of her own identity. She would take her fulfillment from
her role as wife, from the activities and goals of her husband,
and subsequently those of her children. Largely influenced by
Freud's early formulation of penis envy as primary in women's
identifications, Deutsch seemed to have ignored her own experience as an assertive, career-oriented woman (Friedan, 1964).
She and other theoreticians of this century also ignored Freud's
own prediction (Howell, 1981). He stated that a psychology of

women eventually would be developed by women themselves and based on their own experience.

Over the past 15 years, women have begun to realize Freud's prediction. The developing theories of female psychology have yet to make a major impact, however, either on the way that women are seen by others or on the way that women see themselves. Basic community attitudes about women and appropriate female behavior have been unsupportive of change. Biases about what is appropriate female behavior appear even where one would expect a value-free attitude. In a study in the early 1970s, for example, the Brovermans and their colleagues (1970) asked a group of professional psychologists to describe the characteristics of an emotionally healthy person. The descriptions coincided with descriptions the psychologists subsequently gave concerning appropriate behavior in a male. The attributes they ascribed to a healthy woman, lack of assertiveness and passivity, were the same ascriptions they gave as symptoms of emotional ill health. A woman who was assertive or expressive ran the risk of being diagnosed as emotionally disturbed.

Women of today who are 40 years old or older grew up in a society that adhered to this earlier view of women. More often than not, they see themselves as being without power, without the intellectual competence of men, and with a position secondary to that of their husbands. Even a woman who has worked outside the home, even had a career, probably sees herself as the passive, silent partner. Her true vocation is that of wife and mother, taking care of others in a male-dominated world. She learned early to make herself attractive to men so that a man would want to marry her, for her ultimate goal in life was to become a wife and then a mother. She was discouraged from developing a sense of herself as competent in any other role. If she did aspire to a career outside the home, developed intellectual capacities, or was in any way assertive, she was criticized, not only by men but also by other women. Typically, she accepted the idea that her personal status in society would be determined not by her own attributes but by the characteristics of the man she married.

Losing the Role of Wife

"When I was younger," an older widow reminisced, "when we saw a woman alone or with other women, we would ask what was wrong with her. A woman would be ashamed to go out alone." Being in the company of other women often implies that a woman has no man to take her places, and for this she is looked on critically and stigmatized. Women alone may be seen as pitiable failures. The status of being married is sometimes more valued than the quality of the relationship. A widow over 60 described her current position in society as she experienced it: "When I was married, I was Mrs. Donnelly. I was somebody. Now that my husband is dead, I'm nobody!" A woman's sense of self is not invested in who she is but in what she is in relation to someone else—her husband.

The words of a battered woman convey the sense of being unable to function outside of the relationship: "I could not imagine how I could live and support the kids. No matter how bad it got, people looked up to me as Dr. C.'s wife." When a woman values herself only in relation to others, her sense of identity is threatened when her relationships are threatened. She can experience a profound disruption of her very being. When a woman is widowed, she loses her husband, she loses her place in society, and she also loses her sense of who she is. Her name (Mrs. C.) loses its meaning; her name is her designation, her signature, her address, her title. Her name locates her in time and place. She gains a label (widow); a label is an ascription without feelings, placed on an inanimate object.

Lopata (1979) described widowhood as a temporary stage of identity reconstruction. The woman who is widowed needs to give up her former identity, an identity that more often than not she prized. Her new identity of widow has no standing and no personal meaning. This role of widow, according to Lopata, should be only temporary. As Golan (1975) put it, ideally the person moves from role to role, from wife to widow to woman.

The grieving process is rarely articulated in terms of identity loss. At the moment she is widowed, the average woman may have no idea what is happening to her. Only with time will she be aware of what she has lost, and she may be without words for what she is experiencing. While we would anticipate that the disruption would be less profound for a woman who is fulfilled in roles other than that of wife, her disruption may be no less pervasive: "I am a full professor in my department. I always had an active life outside of my family. When my husband died, it took me two years to get into any meaningful work again."

Throughout history, some women have always had egalitarian relationships with their husbands. They have shared resources and had flexibility and mutuality in performing their respective roles in marriage. Today more and more women are entering marriage with the expectation that they will share their lives with their husbands and negotiate equally how they will carry out their respective roles of wife and husband. But even for these women, losing a husband will be a profound disruption. Having relationships that frame one's identity is not necessarily a negative or even a nonfeminist choice. Yet in the political struggle for equality, women have demeaned the institution of marriage, considered it to be a way of keeping women in their place. Another perspective on marriage and identification emerges when we consider marriage as a means of satisfying important social and emotional needs.

Relationships and Identity

No person develops and matures in isolation of others. Being involved in relationships is part of the human condition. From childhood people depend on others for love, guidance, and support. In adulthood, most people will form their own families. Any intimate relationship requires surrendering a certain degree of autonomy and independence, and this is especially necessary when people live together under the same roof, building a shared life. Attachments and affiliations have positive meanings for both men and women throughout the life cycle.

The newborn baby and the very infirm elderly person represent the ultimate in human dependency. The young adult setting out to make his or her own way represents the other extreme—independence. The autonomy that is held up as such a desirable goal for adults may essentially constitute an ideal that is by and large unachievable. In reality, as adults mature and form new families, the shift must be from autonomy to mutuality or interdependence (Loevinger, 1980). Individual development over the whole life cycle often has been characterized in terms of increasing individuation. A well-defined, fully individuated sense of self does not necessarily imply total autonomy and freedom from the need for others. Individuality and interdependence with others actually may be essential to one another. Children must receive love and acceptance before they can see themselves as separate persons. The adult's capacity to care for others and to be involved in any reciprocal relationship is based on an increasingly well-defined sense of self (Kegan, 1982; Loevinger, 1980; Mahler, 1968; Sullivan, 1953). As people become more mature, they can accept more readily the fact that the self is always defined in terms of others (Loevinger, 1980). We are interpersonal, interacting creatures. We spend much of our lives balancing the tensions between our own needs and the needs of others. Over the life cycle, the way a person satisfies these needs in relationship to others will vary, depending on the person's stage of development as child, spouse, or parent and, as will be pointed out later, depending on the person's sex.

Schacter (1959) attempted to specify what stimulates people to affiliate with each other and postulated that a basic human need for approval, support, and prestige can be satisfied only in relationship with others. He observed that people seek each other out when their opinions are shaken and they need help interpreting new social realities. When circumstances bring high anxiety, people will especially seek others like themselves, for legitimation and approbation.

Bowlby's work in the 1940s alerted us to the negative psychological consequences of losing relationships. He postulated that people are instinctually motivated to engage in attachment behavior (Bowlby, 1969–1980). Attachment behavior, as he saw it, is any form of behavior that results in a person's attaining or retaining proximity to some other differentiated and preferred individual and that leads to affectional bonds, or attachments. Usually activated under special circumstances, attachment behavior is expressed in the need to touch or cling. In Bowlby's terms, the formation of a bond is generally described as falling in love, maintaining a bond as loving someone, and losing a bond as grieving over someone. While Bowlby's work contributed greatly to our recognizing the universality of people's need for one another, it tells us little about the nature of relationships and their impact on people's lives.

Weiss (1969) explored the nature and variety of human relationships and observed that people draw on a "fund of sociability" to satisfy their various needs. People, he said, need from others opportunities for nurturance, for obtaining guidance, for reassurance of worth, and for integration in an alliance where they feel secure and attached. Different needs may be satisfied in different relationships. When all these needs are expected to be met in one relationship, such as in a marriage, stress and tension can develop in that relationship. Similarly, if most of these needs are met in one relationship, the loss of that relationship will be isolating.

Maslow (1970) considered the human need for relationships to be universal. Until it is satisfied, a person has difficulty achieving self-actualization. At the same time, the self-actualized person is one who can achieve an interdependent, intimate relationship.

Given that people's needs cannot be met in isolation, and that people have a variety of ways to meet affiliative needs, the question still arises: What are the particular needs that are met in a marriage, for a man or for a woman? Beyond sexual intimacy, people find that marriage offers the satisfaction of daily companionship and intimate personal affection. It gives the partners a framework for organizing their daily lives around each other's needs. Marriage also can express the possibility of immortality, through children. For both husband and wife, marriage is therefore a universally accepted way of meeting important social and emotional needs. Any one marriage may fulfill more or less of these needs, depending upon the social climate and the partners' social class, religious and ethnic backgrounds, and expectations of each other. However, any marriage that works will frame and focus the daily lives of both spouses and also will meet much of their adult need for an intimate relationship. Doing so, the marriage will define, for each partner, a significant part of who they are.

Male and Female Psychology of Relationships

Whether men and women have different approaches to involvements with others is a crucial question in both the study of bereavement and the current theorizing about male and female psychology.

Most studies of affiliation and attachment behavior have been based on men's experiences; consequently, women's behavior and experiences have been understood in comparison with men's rather than in their own terms. The new psychology of women has begun to look more closely and more objectively at women's own experiences in order to distinguish myth from reality. The objective and systematic examination of the ways in which men and women are treated and in turn experience the world is a critical step toward eliminating the judgmental bias that men's experiences are inherently better or more desirable.

Much of the early research in this vein aimed to prove that there are no innate differences between men and women (e.g., Tavris & Offir, 1977). Indeed, based on the foregoing discussion, we might assume that men's needs for others are similar to those of women. However, real differences seem to exist in the way these needs are expressed over the life cycle. These differences may not be simply the result of the legal and social definitions of husband and wife or of man and woman in our society, although these issues cannot be ignored in consideration of recent research. The causes of these differences are complex, largely unresolved, and too extensive to discuss here, but several points will help to elucidate the differences germane to bereavement.

In the first place, men and women may experience their role assignments differently. While the role of husband may give a man an important life framework, his identity is not tied to this role. For a woman, the role of wife is fused with her sense of self. This point receives support from recent research that shows how women generally develop their sense of self out of relationships with others. Men, on the other hand, seem more invested for their identification in their work and achievements.

Levinson and his associates (1978), in their studies of a cohort of adult men, found that in early adulthood men spent most of their energy developing their identities as workers. This was important to them as a way of defining themselves in the larger community. Their relationships with wives and investments in families were secondary. Only as work faded in importance, for example when they approached retirement, did they begin to invest their sense of self in their relationships. Not surprisingly, depression among men seems to result from the loss of a job, the loss of a place in the larger world, losses that challenge their autonomy and independence. For them, autonomy and achievement seem to be the prizes in development, and people who do not achieve or aspire to these objectives are seen as defective (Broverman et al., 1970).

Another dimension of the differences between men's and women's responses to roles and life experience in the context of their relationships emerges in examinations of their views of dominant social values. Kohlberg (1969) has studied men's moral development, the way they develop a sense of right and wrong and of responsibility to self and others. In the middle of his six-part scale, at stage three, morality is measured in interpersonal terms. Here, goodness is associated with helping and pleasing others. In the higher stages of morality, relationships are subordinated to rules, and rules to universal principles of justice. Measured according to this scale, women do not as a group achieve the higher levels of moral development. They seem to be fixed at the middle stage, focusing their responses on their caring for and concern with the needs of others (Gilligan, 1982). In response to questions about moral dilemmas, women focus on the context and its meaning for participants; they aim to avoid hurt; and they consider feelings. Since women had shown less concern for absolute principles of right and wrong, it had been assumed that they could not achieve as high a level of "moral development" as men. Gilligan pointed out that women's values, rather, are embedded in their own relationships with others, and they interpret the meanings of actions in terms of relationship.

Even children show such sex-related differences. School-aged boys at play showed more concern with the rules of the game, arguing them out if need be so the game could continue. Girls were more intent on maintaining relationships among the players, and they would discontinue play rather than argue about the differences that arose among them (Gilligan, 1982).

Most studies of depressed women report that the depression had its onset after the loss of a significant relationship, which contrasts with the findings that men become depressed in relation to the more instrumental aspects of their lives. Summarizing the research in this area, Scarf (1980) wrote, "Important figures leaving or dying; the inability to establish other meaningful bonds with a peer-partner; being forced by a natural transition in life to relinquish an important love tie; a marriage that is ruptured . . . are among the commonest causes of female depression" (p. 95).

Gilligan (1982) has challenged the striving for autonomy and the reference to absolutes as measures of mature adulthood. The sequence of a woman's moral development proceeds from an initial concern with survival, to a focus on goodness, and finally to a reflective understanding of care as the best guide to resolving human conflicts.

> The elusive mystery of women's development lies in its recognition of the importance of attachment in the human life cycle. While developmental theorists have emphasized the importance of autonomy, separation and individuation, women have known the importance of others. However, instead of valuing this quality, they feel criticized for weakness. [Gilligan, 1982, p. 23]

Miller (1976) noted that if women do not achieve, or even seek, the autonomy pursued by men, this should not be viewed as a deficit, but as a healthy, mature, and valuable characteristic. Moreover, the differences observed may not be absolute; they may be matters of emphasis, degree, and timing in the life cycle. For example, some evidence suggests that as a woman relinquishes her child-bearing role and her involvement in raising a family, she may become more involved in work and other instrumental activities. Little is known yet about how much such life cycle changes, including widowhood, alter a woman's focus on relationships, her sense of who she is, or even her dominant social values.

Implications for the Widow

When a widow faces the loss of her role as wife, she faces devastation in her inner and outer being. All her life, relationships have been primary. She has invested in this one relationship particularly. Losing her husband, she loses her role as wife, her special relationship, and a significant part of herself. In her outer being, she loses the social and legal approval for her chosen role as wife. As a widow, she in a sense has a spoiled identity. If she does not appreciate her qualities as a woman, then as a widow who values deeply and now misses profoundly her relationship, she can easily fall into the role of victim. She needs to know that she has to develop a new sense of self, and if she does not know how, she may need to be shown the way.

Many men solve the problem of widowhood by remarrying. Seventy-one percent of elderly men, for example, are married, in contrast to 10 percent of older women. Most women live on as widows for 15 years after their husbands' deaths. To deal with her aloneness and with her twofold loss—her lost relationship and her lost sense of who she is—the widow must let go of the past and also build a new identity. Unless or until she can achieve these goals, she may remain frozen in an outdated self, grieving, mourning, and sometimes becoming depressed. To emerge from these shadows, she must find ways to deal with her loss that will acknowledge its permanent impact on herself and that will recognize the possibility of change and adaptation. Eventually, she must develop new relationships and other identities, new and meaningful roles for herself as a single and formerly married woman.

3 Stages in a Widow's Transition

It will take time for the widow to relinquish her investment in the role of wife, to become accommodated to a new life orientation and patterns of daily living, and to emerge with a redefinition of who she is. In time, although she will not forget the past, she will find new ways of remembering it and different ways of relating to it. Toward these goals, she will encounter several stages, each characterized by different feelings and accommodation tasks. In the transition model we are using, accomplishing the tasks in one stage is seen as facilitating movement to the next stage and to a new level of accommodation. The widow will need some assistance from outsiders, friends, or family in dealing with the pain and disruption of this long transition, in changing her relationship to the past, and in building a future that reformulates the past as a prologue. The following description of how widows have experienced these stages lays the groundwork for the remainder of the book.

Impact: "It Didn't Really Happen, Did It?"

Widows usually report that numbness envelops them when they are told that their husbands have died. They feel a sense of unreality and disbelief, and their behavior becomes still and robotlike. The widow's new legal status as a widow has no social and emotional meaning to her. Automatically, she thinks, feels, and acts as her husband's wife, still tailoring her behavior, as she probably did while he was alive, to her perception of what would please him. Continuing to play the role of wife, she knows how to behave and what is expected of her. Her numbness helps her to perform her role reflexively.

The intensity and duration of a widow's numbness will vary depending on whether her husband died suddenly or after a long illness. When death follows a long illness, the widow inevitably has a certain sense of relief, and the shock is not as profound as when death comes as a surprise. This widow's social and emotional resources probably have been drained by caring for her husband, and she is likely to feel exhausted and near collapse now that her vigil has ended:

> I came home from the hospital. The children sensed that it was over and my son started crying. For three weeks we had known that he could not live. The children and I lay down, and for the first time since we knew, we slept through the night.

When the husband's death is sudden and totally unexpected, the widow's shock and numbness are likely to be pervasive. She has not had time to say goodbye, to think about being alone, or to make even the most rudimentary and tentative plans. The fact that death comes so suddenly strengthens the disbelief characteristic of this stage:

> I wasn't there when he died. I kept thinking he was on vacation. If I could have been there, I think it would have helped make it more real. Other widows have told me that they couldn't believe it for months and that even a year later they would forget and think of their husbands as alive.

Many widows have no idea how to arrange a funeral or even what sort of observance they want to have:

> I didn't know what to do. I didn't even know how to get him from the hospital to a funeral home. I remembered that my cousin was a widow and I called her. Fortunately she came right over and took charge. She made a few calls and things started to happen.

If the husband and wife had discussed funeral arrangements before his death, the widow may have fewer decisions to make at this painful time, but she may have other difficult problems to face:

He didn't want a big wake with an open coffin. His mother was very upset but I insisted on honoring his wishes. I didn't think I had the strength to argue. I never stood up to anyone like that before. It was almost as if I were suddenly a different person—a part of me was somehow closed off. But I had to do what he wanted. I was his wife. I owed it to him.

The widow with little children has the problem of deciding how much to involve them in the funeral ceremonies. Usually, she has had no preparation for these decisions:

I always regretted that I wouldn't let my five year old come to the funeral. Everyone kept saying she was too young. It wasn't until later that I realized that she was more frightened by what she imagined went on than she would have been seeing what actually happened.

Sometimes she finds the older children a source of strength and knowledge at this time:

My son has had a whole discussion at Sunday School about funerals and cemeteries. I couldn't believe it. I hadn't paid any attention. Now he was telling me what would happen. He wasn't frightened or anything. He was 14 and was able to explain what was going on to his younger brother. They decided it would be right for them to come to the funeral. I needed them and they wanted to say goodbye to their father.

The numbness of this stage can be a valuable asset in averting a state of collapse. One widow recalled how it helped her through the details of arranging the funeral:

You have to be out of it a bit. How else could you go through the motions of selecting burial clothes and even choosing a coffin? If I

hadn't been I could never have stood the pain of the fact that this
was for my husband.

Although the numbness may temporarily protect the
widow from the most acute anguish, it does not necessarily
blind her to other people's reactions. While organizing and
participating in the funeral, she may become aware for the first
time since her husband's death of other people's fears that she
may break down and behave irrationally:

> The doctor kept insisting that I take a tranquilizer. He said that my
> family was afraid I'd break down at the funeral. It would have been
> numbing the already numb. I was so angry I almost did become
> irrational at that point. Now I realize that it wasn't really me they
> were worried about—they just didn't know how they were going to
> deal with me, if I really did let go.

Most women are grateful that someone else is willing to
think for them at this time, and this is the time when people are
available to help. They can help arrange the funeral, help with
shopping and housekeeping chores, or chauffeur the children to
visit friends. At a time when she is least able, the widow must
begin dealing with a complex of financial issues, and others may
be able to help with these matters as well. She has to find out
about her insurance, collect back pay, determine what money
she has for current expenses, apply for Social Security and
veterans' benefits, and, if there is an estate, deal with the lawyer.

Some things only she can handle. Eventually she will have
to go to bed in the empty bedroom, see her husband's belong-
ings around her, eat alone, and deal, by herself, with household
routines. The older woman whose children have their own
homes may be able to postpone confronting these changes for
an extended period of time:

> I slept on the living room couch and ate at my children's every
> night. It was almost a year before I came home at supper time. I
> collapsed. I couldn't stop crying. I was sure I was going crazy.

Widows with younger children in the home have no choice
but to carry on, no matter how they feel:

I tried not to cry in front of my children. I wanted things to be as normal as possible for them. Then my little one stopped working at school, and the teacher said he was depressed. The children felt that it wasn't right that things should be the same now that their father was dead. They thought I didn't care about him.

The children were frightened about the future. After the funeral when we ate our first meal alone we were all miserable. You could have cut the silence with a knife. No one wanted to sit in my husband's chair. Finally I did. Then I made a list of chores that needed doing. I don't know where I got the strength. Everyone got a job to do. My oldest started to cry and left the table. When he came back we knew we would survive.

The impact stage has no set duration. Nor is it a purely numb period without any breakthrough of feelings. But the fact that the widow has many concrete chores, including difficult ones such as planning the funeral, involves her in necessary and important activities, keeps her engaged in the real world, and yet allows her some time before the full meaning of what has happened enters her consciousness. The many people who are available to help at this time may be deceived by her outward reactions. They think that she is doing well, and they are pleased, with her, about how well she is holding up. They are unaware, and she also may not recognize, that this is but the first stage in a long and painful process.

Recoil: "I Thought I Was Doing Fine, and Now Everything Is Falling Apart"

As the numbness wears off, most widows fight its departure. With the return of feelings comes the full realization of the loss. They have avoided the meaning of the loss, and may continue to do so as their new reality intermittently breaks through:

My husband had been dead for six months. I was job hunting. The first time I had to check "widow" on a form I had to hold my hand because it started to shake. Until then I had avoided saying that word or even thinking of myself as a widow.

When the widow's normal feelings begin to reemerge, she may experience fright, despair, hollowness, even anger:

> We'd built a good life together. Then it was taken away. I felt so cheated. I kept saying, "Why us?" as if anyone had a good answer.

It is not unusual at this stage for the widow to feel as though a part of herself has been amputated. She may experience a loss of appetite, or sleeplessness, or, conversely, a desire to eat or sleep all of the time. She may find herself impatient and restless, not wanting to be with people but not wanting to be alone either. She may begin to feel increasingly misunderstood, that friends and relatives are becoming impatient and uncomfortable with her continuing grief. Some women feel that if they can simply keep themselves so busy that they grow too tired to do anything except fall into bed, they will be able to keep their feelings at bay and that they can avoid thinking about either the past or the future.

The widow's life still may seem totally unreal, as she imagines that her husband has only gone away on a trip. She may hear his footsteps at the door, especially at the hour he normally would return from work. She may sense his presence in the room:

> I used to hear his car pull in the driveway. I used to look at the drivers of cars that were like his, trying to see if my husband was behind the wheel. I'd go to the mall and look at all the faces going by, looking for him. Every time I went to church I would feel an incredible sadness, for a long, long time. I would picture his casket in the aisle. My list is endless.

Many widows review the circumstances of their husbands' deaths over and over again, wondering whether anything could have been done. Feelings of anger and remorse are not unusual. The widow may feel angry that her husband did not take better care of himself. She may feel remorseful that she did not do enough. At some point she will have to accept philosophically that "his time had come," whether her husband was a young man or not.

A hundred times I said to myself, "If only I had insisted that we go to the doctor the week before. If only . . ." I would drive myself crazy and anyone else who would listen to me. I kept rewriting the script, but there was no way I could get back the happy ending.

The widow whose marriage has not been totally satisfactory may feel guilt over her relief in not having to deal any more with the unpleasantness of the marriage. Grown children may pose problems, and they sometimes become overprotective. Sometimes they are having trouble dealing with their own grief:

My daughter flew in from California. She began to run my life, telling me how I would manage now. The next thing I knew she was talking about picking me up and moving me out there with her. I don't know where I got the energy—I was still in a daze—but I sat her down and I made it clear to her that I could run my own life. I appreciated that her job was to be helpful. I also understood that she had lost her father, and I thought perhaps she had some crying to do. I was right. It was her way of not facing her own grief. We both had a good cry and then I could talk to her as a friend about what I was really going to do now. I did need her advice.

My son worried me. He never talked about his father. He was away at school. He came home and without saying a word he took a leave of absence from school and got a job. I was glad to have him around. He did not cry; he did not talk. He just needed to be there. When he decided to go back to school, we were both ready for him to leave. We never really talked about his feelings, but we didn't need to.

The widow is generally not prepared for the miserable feelings she begins to experience. She has to discover that there is no easy way around her misery, given the nature and meaning of her loss. If she knows that her suffering is normal and inevitable, she may find it easier to endure:

I was so proud of myself. I thought I was doing so well. I thought that I had everything under control. I was starting to look for a job. And all of a sudden the bottom fell out. I started to cry when my neighbor called "good morning" to me. I began yelling at my daughter on the phone when she called. No one had warned me I might feel this way. I called the doctor and he offered me a tranquilizer. Then I spoke to another widow. She was great. She said it was normal. Once I appreciated that I was bound to have bad days and even bad weeks, I didn't need the tranquilizers any more.

At this stage, when the widow most needs reassurance and support, she may find herself more and more alone:

For a while my life was so crowded that I needed a traffic cop. Suddenly I was all alone. I guess I had become the fifth wheel people talk about.

Friends and relatives who have observed how well she is doing may assume that she is over the worst of her grief and beginning to "recover." They have their own lives to lead, they become impatient with any continuing need the widow may express, and ultimately they cannot face the grief themselves. When family and friends do remain available and supportive, therefore, their attention may not be helpful. They will often try to help by distracting her from her grief, but the grief is what she needs to experience at this stage. Only when the widow can at last acknowledge her pain, her doubts, her fears, only when she no longer feels she must present a false picture of how splendidly she is coping, only then can she begin to make the necessary changes toward accommodation. And yet she herself may not understand that she needs to change:

You have to go through the stage where you feel that if you don't have a man to get up for in the morning, what's it for? I felt like half a person. At that time my own goals weren't enough. When the kids left, I had the same feelings, but it was different. I needed them and they needed me, but not in the same way.

Although she does not yet articulate the components of a new identity, the widow begins to see the direction in which she has to go. She has a mental outline of life as a formerly married, single woman:

> I had never thought of myself doing any of those things—balancing my checkbook, buying a house, negotiating a loan.

She begins to see the need for new friends and new relationships. At the end of this stage, she has the courage to say,

> I realized that I had to accept a new image of myself. My world was different now, and no matter how much I may have wished that I could go backwards, it was not going to happen that way.

Accommodation: "There Seems to Be a Light at the End of the Tunnel"

The widow now begins to discover new ways of looking at the world. Entering this stage does not mean the end of depressed feelings or an end to the pain of her loss. These feelings do become less intense and pervasive, and she has a different perspective on her experience:

> I very often give the impression that I have it all together, but I really don't. It is a constant struggle and the only way I get by is one day at a time. In the final analysis, I still have trouble believing that he is gone, but I do know that I can't change what happened. Life is either lived, half lived, or shelved. I either have to stagnate or go on. It's my choice. We all have the potential and ability to change. It's my decision. We can win or lose depending on our attitude. To lose means to end up totally alone. To have a "win" attitude means that all sorts of avenues can open up and there will be green lights all the way.

She learns that she can laugh and that she has things worth living for; she can enjoy people and look forward to getting up in the morning. She can look upon her husband and her past without despairing of her present or her future. Remembering that past, she can cry without becoming frightened or uncomfortable about it, without worrying about other people's reactions. She accepts the fact that part of her will always be sad when she thinks about the past, and she considers this natural and right. The happiest occasions can evoke the greatest sadness:

> When my daughter received her cap in nursing, it was very exciting for me. There was the pride I felt watching her walk up on the stage, but there was also the shattering sense of loss I experienced not having her father there. He idolized her and he was not there to share her day, and he doesn't know the fine young man who is her husband.

> They had a ceremony for parents when the boys graduated from Cub Scouts to Boy Scouts. My son showed off some of the work he had done. His father would have been so proud. I had to work at keeping back the tears. In fact we both cried a bit. I told him that his father would have been so pleased. He beamed at that, and it made the evening for him.

The widow needs to remember. Her ways of remembering are her ways of honoring her dead husband and of building continuity between her past and her future. Some widows set up memorial funds, some donate flowers annually on their husbands' birthdays, some become active in a project or area that was important to him. Others make scrapbooks, or carefully store those personal possessions that their children will use when they are older.

Repopulating her life with new friends and becoming involved in work are ways of building new identities and new roles for herself. She begins to change the old habits of daily living that framed her life and develops new ones appropriate to her current situation. She finds ways to take charge of her own life:

> My job was routine and boring. I knew I needed a job where I was needed and where someone was counting on me. I had worked with my husband as an editor, but never for money. I thought maybe I could do that again. I decided that a university might be a place for a mature woman. I was right. I work for the math department. I do some editing, correspondence, and generally keep the place going. I work for a group of people who are friendly and supportive and who need me.

I was scared to death. Who would hire a 50-year-old woman who has not worked for 20 years? Someone suggested the telephone company. I took my heart in my hands and went in. They were delighted. They knew I needed the work and could be counted on. There is an advantage in being older, and I found a whole new circle of friends.

The widow needs friends with whom she can share both the good and the bad times, who are free when she is free. She finds ways to include her old friends in her new life and does not necessarily wait for them to take the initiative. She begins to date and discovers that remarriage is only one way to overcome her loneliness. She begins to understand that she cannot find a substitute for what she has lost and that remarriage or any new relationship means building something entirely new. But her new sense of self is not simply a reflection of her new relationships with others. She finds a new center to herself, and this gives her a new sense of competence. Proud of her ability to direct her own life, to run her household, and perhaps to raise her children alone, she may also manage a job. She still needs people and is still involved with them in caring relationships, but her new sense of self is not solely dependent upon her ability to be a wife or mother. Even though she might never have chosen to give up her role as a wife, she is beginning to find pleasure in her new independence:

I'm doing things I never thought I could do. I hate being alone, but I have good friends, and we care about each other. I'm even traveling, and I enjoy my work. I never thought I'd hear myself say that I don't mind being single.

To facilitate her movement through the transition, to make her accommodation, the widow needs to learn new skills and new ways to relate to the world. One of the few places from which this kind of expertise is available is in mutual-help groups. The next chapter describes the development of these groups and their special relevance to the problems of the widowed.

4 Mutual Help and Transitions

Among the bases of a stable and just society are the people's convictions that others care and that they are shaping their own destiny. Social justice means nothing more than the simple idea that we owe to others as well as to ourselves. From biblical to early Christian times, performing acts of caring and concern for our fellow human beings has been a cornerstone in the foundation of our Western society. In more recent times, one writer has expressed this metaphorically: "When a man is singing and cannot lift his voice, and another comes and sings with him, another who can lift his voice, the first will be able to lift his voice too. That is the secret of the bond between spirits" (Meyers, 1976, Introduction).

Over the past 200 years or so, this principle has been diluted by the undiscriminating reliance on professionalism. Medicine has made remarkable strides in recent years, and professional expertise has emerged as the panacea for every disturbance to which mankind is subject. This has blurred the distinction between illness, where a professional person is truly required and helpful, and those disturbances that arise in the course of normal life transitions, where ordinary people can be helpful. As Friedson has observed, "A pathology arises when outsiders may no longer evaluate the work by rules of logic and the knowledge available to all educated men, and when the only legitimate

45

spokesman on an issue relevant to all men must be someone who is officially certified" (1970, p. 92). The pathology Friedson refers to is that people essentially have been disenfranchised from solving their own problems. People today are being taught that in times of stress they need to consult an expert. Success in coping based on a person's life experience counts for nothing, and experiential knowledge has little value. Help is systematized, roles are sharply defined between consumer and professional in bureaucratic agencies, and the recipients of help often feel dehumanized.

A countertrend to this untoward professionalism is developing in the quiet revolution among would-be consumers of organized human services. Fully realized, this revolution would change the very nature of these services. Over the past decade, mutual-help groups and organizations have proliferated, involving consumers directly in the delivery of services and using their own experience with a critical problem as the basis of help. Consumers themselves control the way that help is provided as well as the workings of the service organization. Informally and often spontaneously, people have rediscovered the value of learning from peers who have experienced a similar problem and who have coped successfully. These mutual-help efforts value the resources that people have within themselves, to help themselves and to help reach others. More significantly, these efforts are demonstrating that mutual help is sometimes the most appropriate and relevant help. Mutual help is therefore not simply a reaction against professional help but also a positive and sometimes superior response to human need.

One of the most extensive mutual-help networks is that which is evolving among bereaved people. The largest group of bereaved persons are the widowed. Many of these efforts follow the model developed through the Widow-to-Widow program. Widowed helpers reach out to the newly widowed people in a target community, offering friendship, guidance, and support and sharing their own experiences. The idea has proliferated in the past two decades in part because of the direct match between the needs of the newly widowed and the content and framework of mutual help.

The Nature of Mutual Help

On any given day, a person usually participates in many helping exchanges involving different people around different issues. These interactions occur in the family, in the neighborhood, at work, and with friends and peers. Babysitting arrangements, food cooperatives, and family associations represent examples of formal networks; helping exchanges also can be unplanned and spontaneous. Most human life is barren without these exchanges. Kropotkin (1902) proposed that cooperation and mutual aid are the very essence of the human condition and that they make a society viable. The variety of helping networks in which a given individual participates can be described in terms of the problems at hand and the actors involved.

Helping exchanges take many forms. Formally trained helpers such as clergy members, teachers, police, physicians, and social workers give help because it is their job. Although they usually charge some fee for services, they do not expect direct reciprocity. Others help because of their relationship to each other, such as parents and children, husbands and wives, and neighbors. These helping exchanges are usually reciprocal, and they occur in part because people feel a sense of obligation and responsibility to and for each other. Still others, out of a sense of altruism, help as volunteers in organized efforts in community agencies.

A mutual-help exchange involves people who share a common problem, a problem that one of the people previously has coped with successfully. The helping person has expertise based on personal experience and the ability to solve a particular problem. Life experience as the basis for offering help contrasts with the formal education that is the professional helper's base of expertise.

A mutual-help network may become formal and evolve into a systematic organization and program. Although these organizations have been called *self-help* organizations, the help invariably goes to others as well as to oneself, so the term *mutual help* seems more appropriate. Of course a helper, in the process of helping, may work out some aspect of his or her own difficulty, obtain new perspectives, and get a renewed sense of self-adequacy from discovering the capacity to help someone else. Self-help is a first step; the individual becomes aware of the problem and then tries to do something about it. Once the individual engages someone else in sharing experiences, then it becomes mutual help.

Alcoholics Anonymous (AA) is one of the best-known mutual-help groups. Only a former alcoholic who has been dry for a period of time and who was helped by the AA method can become a helper. Helpers are not recruited from professional schools; their expertise comes from their own success in coping with alcoholism. AA relies on indigenous talents and resources for its success. A mutual-help organization limits its membership to individuals with a designated common problem. Their purpose in coming together is to offer one another help and guidance in solving their common problems or mutual predicaments.

Sharing of experience is the fundamental concept distinguishing mutual help from other helping exchanges. The essence of the exchange is a peer relationship. By its very nature, the patient–doctor or the client–worker relationship is unequal, with the patient or client in a subordinate position. The exchange entails no reciprocity, and the model generally holds that people without the requisite training cannot help with emotional problems and in fact can do harm (Levine & Levine, 1970).

When a group becomes formalized, in order to maintain its character as a mutual-help organization, it must develop an organizational structure, with officers, a governing body, and procedures for continuity. The members determine all policy and control all resources, and they are also both providers and recipients of service. Membership is limited to people who have the particular problem or problems with which the group is concerned. Mutual-help organizations must be distinguished from such voluntary philanthropic organizations as the American Cancer Society, where volunteers usually join in order to help others, not to solve a common problem. Mutual-help groups maintain their identity because of the shared experiences and commitments of their members around the problems that brought them together.

The Evolution of Mutual-Help Groups

Informal mutual exchanges go on all the time, as people discover in each other common experiences that until that moment they may have believed were theirs alone. Sometimes people seek out someone who they know has had a similar experience, or they are introduced by a common friend. These exchanges usually do not move beyond the level of informal encounters. When informal encounters do develop into formal clubs or organizations, it may occur because people in the group sense they have a mission to extend their discovery to others like them. Or it may happen because the interest is so great that the number of potential members cannot be absorbed into an informal network.

Mutual Help in Human Services

In some instances, mutual-help organizations have sprung up when their founders shared the experience of inadequate, inappropriate, or unsuccessful professional help. Professional failure was a motivating force in the foundation of several very large organizations, including AA and the Associations for Retarded Citizens. Founders of these groups had been treated unsuccessfully for many years in clinical programs. Retarded children were relegated to institutions; parents were advised that their children had no place in society and would be better off apart from it. Parents often were treated as if they were sick: having a retarded child meant they needed psychiatric assistance. Effective programs for these populations have grown out of the sufferers' own efforts and their discovery, through one another, of meaningful solutions to their problems.

The greatest number of such organizations—although not encompassing the majority of members—have been formed by people with physical illness or handicaps. Because of advances in medical science, many people are alive today who even 10 years ago would not have survived. Advanced technology has solved the tragic problem of some early deaths but has created problems in the quality of life for the new survivors. Motivated by their desire to continue living and their wish to improve the quality of their lives, many of these people have begun to solve their own problems by working together, often in collaboration with health professionals.

Mutual Help and Social Change

Yet another impetus for mutual help is the nature of our rapidly changing society. During periods of rapid social change, established patterns of reaction and coping are no longer adequate. Gaps develop quickly between familiar old patterns of coping and the challenges posed by new conditions. Such gaps emerge in the aftermaths of devastating wars, in the impacts of new technologies that first spawned the industrial revolution and now bring the age of automation and computers, and in the challenges that accompany any new knowledge about the universe and human behavior. Changes such as these are occurring with greater speed and in greater numbers than ever before. We live in an age of instant communication. We are bombarded constantly with new information and new technologies. The way we live, the food we eat, the entertainment we enjoy, the way we understand each other's behavior—all are changing. Not only are the things we talk about different, but the ways we communicate are different. Telecommunications leaves little time between a new discovery and its dissemination; however, there are time lags between the broadcasting of new knowledge and the application of this knowledge by professionals and consumers. Professional help suddenly can become outdated.

The patterns of behavior, the traditions, and the divisions of labor that worked well in the not-so-distant past are not necessarily relevant today. In the past, the family oriented its members, preparing them with reactions, values, and behavior patterns for coping with the outside world. A son who learned to

behave like his father, or a daughter like her mother, was prepared to deal with the larger community. Today this is no longer
true. With the rapidly occurring social changes on the outside,
the family cannot keep up with its members' needs and is losing
its function as the major interpreter of society and educator of
future generations. As a result, people have more challenges as
they move through the normal transitions in the life cycle occa-
sioned by birth, death, marriage, and so forth. People do not
automatically know how to behave as they move from one role
to another, from one experience to another, in the shifting norms
of the larger society.

Mutual-help groups have begun to fill this void. They are
places where people can go to amass their common experience
and to evolve more effective modes of coping with their problems in today's world. Mutual-help groups may thus be seen as
enabling individual adaptation during periods of change. As
they help people to learn to behave differently in different roles
at a time of transition, they are enabling organizations. In short,
their purpose is to get people from here to there, for example
from a hospital bed back to the community and leading as
normal a life as possible (Lenneberg, 1970). In essence an individual moves through various stages of transition in order to
achieve an accommodation. Help at each of these stages must
differ according to the changing needs of, for example, the
widow.

What are the qualities, in the context in which a particular
transition is played out, that become central to achieving an
accommodation? What are the characteristics of helpers that
make them most effective? There is a body of data that emphasizes the special value of helpers who have been through a
similar experience. There is evidence that learning in crises or
emotionally laden situations is enhanced in a peer context (Bandura, 1977). Reporting on a study of affiliative tendencies in
college students during periods of anxiety, Stanley Schacter
(1959) observed that subjects chose to be alone under stress
rather than with people who did not share their experience. He
concluded that, whatever the needs aroused by anxiety, it seems
that satisfaction demanded the presence of others in a similar
situation. In a small sample of members of three mutual-help

groups—Kidney Transplant and Dialysis Association, the Cured Cancer Club, and the Spina Bifida Association of Massachusetts—I found that people who joined these groups did so out of a pressing need to find someone else who had had a similar experience, with whom they could share feelings and discover new ways of coping (Silverman & Smith, 1984).

Roxanne Silver and Camille Wortman (1980) noted that peers (those who have been through the same experience) are unique sources of help for people in stress. They are more understanding and patient, and their expectations are more appropriate. The impact of learning from peers as an important source of information, experience, and assistance with transition needs to be appreciated and further examined. As children grow, we recognize their need to learn from peers who serve as role models or with whom they can explore ways of coping with their common needs (Rubin, 1980). Children who have role-model peers do not feel alone, unique, or isolated; they feel legitimated. This type of relationship probably pertains to an entire lifetime and not just to childhood and adolescence.

Not only is the need to find someone like oneself central to making a critical transition, but the opportunity to change roles and become a helper may be important as well. A survey was conducted comparing two groups: (1) the members of a group of heart patients called Mended Hearts and (2) a group of heart surgery patients not affiliated with the organization (Lieberman & Borman, 1979). The investigators' desire was to determine how participation in the group affected people's adjustment to their illness. It was found that significant differences appeared between the two groups only among retired men who were active in the organization. Those who became helpers made the best adjustment to open-heart surgery. The role of helper tends to foster competency in the helper. In addition, receiving help from a peer tends to minimize a sense of weakness or incompetence in the person needing help. I am suggesting that during periods of transition, when people must obtain relevant new information in order to cope, their ability to use this information is affected by the availability of someone who has gone through the experience, with whom the individual can identify. In addition, the opportunity to change roles from recipient to helper further enhances the accommodation. The context in which help occurs is critical in terms of the personal experience of the helper and the opportunities within the helping framework for mutuality and role mobility. When role mobility is considered, it is important to look at the dynamic issues in any helping exchange. Since transitions take place over time, available help must change over time also.

Mutual Help and the Stages of Transition

Robert Lifton (1973), in a study of experiences of returning Vietnam veterans, identified factors in the helping situation that facilitate coping with a transition. He found three essential qualities: The first is that of *affinity*, the coming together of people who share a particular, and in this case overwhelming, historical personal experience, along with a basic perspective on that experience, who wish to make some sense of it. The second quality is that of *presence*, a kind of being there or full engagement and openness to mutual impact, with no one ever being simply a therapist, or a person acting as a neutral sounding board. The third factor was that of *self-generation*, the need on the part of those seeking help, change, or insight to initiate their own process and conduct it largely on their own terms. Even when calling in others with expert knowledge, those who seek help retain major responsibility for the shape and direction of the enterprise. Affinity, presence, and self-generation seem to be necessary ingredients for making a transition between old and new images and values, particularly when these relate to ultimate concerns, to ultimate concerns of life and death.

A parallel can be drawn between the unfolding of a mutual-help exchange and the stages of transition. Drawing this parallel seems a good way of summarizing the unique aspects of mutual help in aiding people through transition, and of demonstrating how helping relationships must change over time.

The first stage of a transition is the impact/affinity stage. People are preoccupied with a desire to reject the new situation. Ability to make an accommodation depends upon allowing the numbness to lift and recognizing at some level that a new reality exists. This becomes easier to do when someone is available who has been in the same situation, is now living a normal life, and is even able to help others. An affinity develops that makes it possible for a bond to grow between seeker and helper. New members are then less fearful about their new situation.

For new members, willingness to talk with such a helper is an indication of readiness to consider making a transition, to learn to accept a new status and role designation. For example, a woman who agrees to talk about her widowhood with another widow begins to cast off her feeling of numbness and to see that this designation may apply to her. Although she still may not be ready to call herself "widow" and to accept the full meaning of her husband's death for her current life, she will find guidelines in the new exchange. The first question she will ask is, "What happened to you? How did you get here?" The helper must be prepared to retell her story.

In the recoil/presence stage, the second phase of transition, help consists of the provision of specific information about the condition and/or new role and about how to deal with it effectively. The person in transition is able to accept this information because of the presence or unity that has developed.

Either in one-to-one contact or at group meetings, advice is offered about how to deal with a problem or what to expect from the situation that the sufferer is experiencing. A framework is provided for the problem. Not only does she or he learn to understand the current experience, but she or he may receive anticipatory guidance about problems that will arise. For example, a newly bereaved woman does not know that she will even be able to stop crying or ever feel joy again. She learns how others have dealt with the problem, and they share with her their tricks of the trade. Such interactions serve to expand her coping repertoire and options.

The content of the help inevitably will differ with the problem. The information offered has to relate to the specific transition, but once people have found a way of talking to each other, what is it that is talked about? Much of what mutual aid is about is the small things. It's not the big deal, the surgery (that is, the important lifesaving experience or whatever else it might be); it's the small, survival-oriented kinds of things that make up the essence of daily life (Lenneberg, 1971).

Accommodation/self-generation is the third stage of transition. Accommodation is a period in which the individual's feelings have quieted down and the person is beginning to integrate new knowledge into a new identity. This time is used for practicing new behavior patterns, new ways of dealing with oneself and the world. Accommodation can be likened to an active apprenticeship period. During this time the moral support of the group may be essential for success as a person integrates the past with the present.

In this period the new member moves out of the new-member status and becomes aware of and responsive to other people's needs. The option of becoming a helper is now available. In order to be helpful in turn, either in an informal exchange or as part of an organized effort, the helper has to control resources and be able to integrate into the helping activity the knowledge gained from the experience. The context in which the help is offered becomes critical. It is not only the type of help itself that distinguishes mutual help from other kinds of help, but it is also the setting in which the work is carried out and the helper's relationship to that system. At a time of transition, then, the goal of help is to assist the individual in moving from one role to another, from one status to another. This is the work the widow has to do, and it is the thesis of this book that her work is facilitated by her participation in a temporary community of other widows, that is, in a mutual-help group.

II

An Overview of the Widow-to-Widow Project

5 History of the Widow-to-Widow Project

Early Goals

In 1964 when I began my work with the widowed, mutual help for the bereaved was a rare phenomenon. Gerald Caplan, who was then the Director of the Laboratory of Community Psychiatry at Harvard Medical School, had asked me to determine what types of intervention might be most helpful to the newly widowed. In particular, he suggested that we identify an intervention that would prevent the development of major psychiatric disorder in the widowed population. Psychiatric wisdom at the time suggested that bereavement placed the widowed person at risk of developing serious emotional difficulties (Parkes, 1965), and studies indicated that younger women had especially serious difficulties when their husbands died (Maddison & Viola, 1967; Marris, 1958).

Following the public health model, we aimed to find an intervention that could be directed to the whole population at risk. While psychological illness is certainly not the fate of every bereaved person, it is not always possible to identify in advance those individuals who will break down. To reach those who had special need, we would need to reach every widowed person. Our model for intervention thus would be somewhat like a program of vaccination in which everyone is immunized, even those who might have a natural immunity.

The Search for a Strategy

This mandate required addressing a number of preliminary questions: What services were already available in the community for the widowed? What services did they actually use? What were their actual needs that, if unmet, might lead to subsequent problems? How could these needs be met? I especially wondered whether a new service was needed or whether something might be done with those that already existed. At the time, I did not even consider that a program might be run by the widowed for the widowed, although I did recognize that services had to be acceptable to the newly widowed and likely to be used. Initially, my idea was to set up a professional program that would be designed to be especially relevant.

Professional Mental Health Perspectives

My interviews with directors and selected staff from a representative sample of psychiatric and social agencies revealed that widowed people made little use of their services. Most of these practitioners believed that making their traditional counseling services available to the bereaved was sufficient. They believed that the best service for the bereaved, as for anyone experiencing an emotional disruption, was to enter into a therapeutic relationship where they could work through their feelings. As they saw it, the critical issues that the bereaved person needed to face were anger and guilt over what had happened.

My review of several agencies' current caseloads showed but one or two widowed people on each caseload (marital status was evident from the face sheet). When these few widowed people had come to the psychiatric agencies, it was often two years after the loss, and grief was not identified by either the person or the agency as the presenting problem. When a widow asked for help, she most often would describe a general malaise and depression that were preventing her from mobilizing her resources. Since the death had occurred two years earlier, its relevance to her current situation was lost. When children were the focus of a widow's referral, some reference might appear regarding a parent's death, but this was rarely a central theme in either the intake or the treatment plan. Agency records of treatment sessions showed that many therapists could not deal with the widow's intense pain and, unaware of this reaction, they often would change the subject.

In 1964, mental health and human services agencies and professionals had yet to discover the problems associated with death and bereavement. Even today, however, we have little reason to believe that many of these professionals would be any more responsive to the needs of the bereaved. The focus of current interest has been on the dying experience rather than on the needs of the living. Many professionals today, as in 1965, tend to take an egocentric view of the world: If they stand ready to serve, they are meeting the need. They fail to recognize that each crisis or transition may involve different needs in response to different intrinsic problems; that is, the needs of the bereaved are different from the needs of the dying. Each set of needs varies and so may require very different services and additional skills that may not exist in the professional community.

Perspectives of Widowed People

I wondered how the widowed themselves saw their needs and how they dealt with their needs. In their study of how Americans view their mental health, Gurin et al. (1960) found that most people went to friends, family, clergy, and physicians for help with what they characterized as their problems in living. Going to mental health professionals and characterizing a problem as a reflection of some inner psychological difficulty was less typical, occurring primarily in urban regions and among people with more than a high-school education. Other studies (Meyers & Timms, 1969; Silverman, 1969a) had found discrepancies between the way a mental health or family agency client characterized his or her problem and the way the professional saw the difficulty. Since clients and professionals also did not agree on what help would be most relevant, clients very often dropped out after the initial visit. These findings supported my interest in finding out how potential consumers viewed their problematic situations.

My telephone survey to a widowed population revealed that they sought help from friends and family. They felt that their pain was something they had to live with and that psychiatric treatment was for people with psychological problems, which did not apply to their situation (Silverman, 1966). Maddison and Walker (1967) found that widowed people who turned to clergy and physicians for help were usually disappointed. My findings were similar. Clergy and physicians seemed to lack the skills for dealing in depth with bereavement. Widows in my survey reported that clergy's usual message, "It was God's will," was little consolation early in the bereavement. The physician's typical statement, "Time will heal," and the prescription of tranquilizers may have lightened the pain in the short run but helped not at all in the long run. The widows reported to me that funeral directors were most helpful at first because they knew what to do when the death occurred; later on, other widowed people were most helpful because they understood what the widow was experiencing.

Funeral Directors

After interviewing the widows themselves, my next step was to contact the caregivers the widow would encounter immediately after the death. I visited several funeral homes to learn what they did and what services they provided.

When a husband dies, the first person a widow has to deal with is the funeral director. Funeral directors clearly offer one essential service: No one else can take the body from the place of death and arrange for the burial. In addition, the funeral directors I met were very knowledgeable about rituals and saw themselves as being available to serve the family. They initiated the application for Social Security and generally tried to be helpful. If no one from the clergy was involved, they would call one to officiate at the funeral. Funeral directors often serve several generations in a family and see the family members after the funeral. They reminded me that during this initial period most bereaved people have more helpers around than they know what to do with. They felt that the widow's needs are greatest not immediately after the death, but months later after all the friends and family have gone back into their own lives.

Clergy

I also talked with members of the clergy. Most of them had received no special guidance on how to help the bereaved. They learn how to officiate at a funeral, but nothing more. Generally, if they saw that a bereaved person was coming to church regularly, they would assume that the person was getting along all right. For the most part, clergy members saw no long-term role for themselves with the bereaved. Many were not comfortable with the concept of grief, and several acknowledged that they actually were uncomfortable with bereaved people. Their theology notwithstanding, members of the clergy were not able to deal with the fact that people do indeed die.

The different religious traditions approach death differently. While most Christian traditions focus on preburial rituals and offer no guidance for the bereaved after the burial, the Jewish tradition gives the bereaved person guidance for mourning behavior over the first year after the death. (The Jewish funeral director pointed out, however, that most Jewish families are unaware of this tradition.)

Other Caregivers

Besides funeral directors, clergy, family, and friends, the other caregivers that widows must meet shortly after the death are Social Security employees, lawyers, and husbands' employers. Social Security employees are only interested in her filling out forms to determine her benefits. She may need to deal with a lawyer to probate the will. She may have to negotiate with her husband's employer for back pay or death benefits. If she has no income, she may have to apply for public welfare.

The Pivotal Idea of Transition

I soon recognized that the widow's needs change over time and that different services would be required in responding to these changing needs. At about this time, I read the articles by Tyhurst (1958) and Bowlby (1961) and found that the concept of transition they described was helpful to my understanding of what I had observed. A critical aspect of help would be to facilitate the change process itself. "Recovery" was not an achievable goal. The focus of any help would have to be on the widow's ability to allow herself to change, to make an accommodation, to accept the fact that she could not return to herself and her situation as they were before.

When I looked at services in light of the idea that different needs and tasks would become salient at various stages in the widow's transition, the real service gaps became apparent (Silverman, 1966). For example, at the beginning, when the clergy, funeral director, family, and friends are so apparently available, the widow is generally numb. She often acts by reflex, and the very word "widow" has no meaning, as she and those around her focus on the concrete tasks of the funeral and the initial mourning rituals. Only somewhat later, during what Tyhurst (1958) called recoil, does the meaning of the loss become clear. The widow now recognizes that she cannot live her life as before; it is then that she needs someone to hear her pain, to legitimate her feelings. But by then, family and friends have returned to their own lives, expecting that she will have "recovered" and be able to manage. At this time, she also may really feel the need for concrete help—with finances, with being a single parent, with going to work, with learning to live alone, with managing her extreme and profound feelings. In effect, she must reorder her whole life within an entirely new context.

This would be the time for intervention, when the widow's friends and family have returned to their own lives and when the reality of her widowhood has begun to touch every part of her life. But what type of intervention should it be? Some of the needs I had identified could be met by mental health professionals. Asking for their help, though, would require that the widow label her difficulty as a symptom of a psychological problem, and this would verify her fear of going crazy and the fear that her feelings were not normal but in some way deviant. In addition, most of the needs I had identified could not be met through counseling alone. I concluded that the widow would need a service specifically designed for her.

Mutual Help as a Strategy

I discovered that the only specific services for the widowed in my area were a few mutual-help groups that widows had set up for themselves and one program directed by a widow employed by Sharon Memorial Park, a local cemetery in Sharon, Mass. This program was based at the cemetery's administrative offices and was intended for women whose husbands had been buried at that cemetery. I learned that the program had begun with the observation that women who visited the cemetery would come to the office to talk about their problems and their loneliness. The director, widowed herself, made herself known and available to every widow by sending a condolence letter shortly after the death; two months later, she sent a checklist to suggest the help that they might need. She then would respond by referring them to community agencies and introducing them to other widows she knew. Twice a year she held evening meetings where the widows could meet each other and hear a lecture on an aspect of their current situation, such as living alone, the grief process, managing money, and so forth. Widows associated with this service praised her outreach but felt that the most important part of her help was the opportunity she created for them to meet each other and to make new friends. These widows' message was clear: Their greatest need was to make new friends and to develop new routines for living. Their message and this model of outreach served as a guide in my subsequent planning.

I visited the mutual-help groups. In 1965 I could identify

but four such groups in the entire United States. There was the Post Cana Conference in Washington, D.C., the Naim Conference in Chicago, Parents Without Partners, and a social club in a suburb of Boston. Parents Without Partners had chapters throughout the nation; most of the members were divorced, and only a few chapters had specific programs for the widowed. Each group reached out through personal contacts, church registries and bulletins, or local newspapers. Naim Conference for a time used its parish registry to match the newly widowed with experienced members, by age and circumstances of death. The visit took place about a month after the death, sometimes sooner if necessary, for example, when a woman was pregnant at the time of her husband's death and was due to deliver in six weeks. These programs each had either a professional advisory board or an advisor assigned by the sponsoring church group. Invariably, however, the organizing initiative had come from the widowed themselves, and they made the program decisions and did the helping. The professionals were there to give moral support and to legitimate the organization in the community, but in many ways their role was window dressing, because they did not understand what the widowed were feeling. The limitations of professional knowledge about widowhood and of professional intervention became even clearer as I saw how much we could learn from the widowed. Members of these groups had not only an ability to bypass the professional as a go-between, but a compelling ability to help each other.

In England, a physician's wife had organized and was directing a group for widows called the Cruse Club. Her approach had allowed some aspects of mutual help to develop. The club's newsletter featured widows writing about their personal stories and how they were helped by the opportunity to meet others. Over and over again, they would say the same things I was hearing in the United States: In the peer group for widows, people understood their pain, no one told them to have a stiff upper lip, and they found role models for how to cope. They came away with hope for the future and with solid ideas about how to get there. These observations were supported by Maddison and Viola's (1967) survey finding that another widow is the most effective helper for widowed people.

nce the advisory committee believed that widows
ut to widowers would be misunderstood in this com-
ey advised that, until men could be found to help,
ws be served. They also recommended that, since
omen were at greater risk, and since the community
ad a range of services for the elderly, only women
be included.

women were recruited as helpers, all of whom had
olved in some type of volunteer community work. All
n widowed from two to five years. Since the project
quire a sustained effort in order to determine the feasi-
the idea, the helpers, who became known as widow
ere paid a small salary based on what they could earn
jeopardizing their Social Security. The five women
four with dependent children; only one was over 62;
ere Catholics, one was Protestant (she stayed with the
m only six months), and one was Jewish; one woman was
nd four were white (Silverman, 1967, 1969b).
order to find the new widows we began by obtaining the
certificates from the Department of Health for all men
he community who had died and were under 65. Since
n are generally younger than their husbands, the age of
sbands presumably would help to identify all women who
be eligible, that is, under 60. Next, since religion is not on
eath certificate and both Protestant and Catholic women
served by the same funeral homes, the project asked the
al directors to help with this information. This was the
ning of a long and fruitful relationship that lasted over
fetime of the project (Silverman, 1972) and eventually led
ants from the funeral directors to pay the aides' salaries.
During their first months of work the aides learned about
community and the resources that they might use, decided
to reach out, and considered how widows might react to
r offers of help. They also spontaneously shared with each
er their own experiences of widowhood and how it had
pared them to understand the needs of the new widow.
ey decided to be available to the newly widowed person for
least one year after the death, to visit her or talk with her on
phone as needed. The project furnished each aide with a

The Widow-to-Widow Approach

The problem of what intervention to offer was solved. It would
be a form of what we would come to call mutual help. I
hypothesized that help offered by another widow might be
accepted by the entire widowed population. As was self-evident
to me, this help had to be offered universally, without requiring
the widow to take the initiative of asking. I therefore proposed a
program that would reach out to every newly widowed person
in a community. At the very time that her need might be greatest, the widow would be most stressed and disorganized, too
burdened to seek and find the most appropriate help.

A further stimulus to this approach came from the New
Careers for the Poor program. In order to reach economically
and socially deprived people who did not use the available
human services, they were sending out as helpers people whose
main qualities were their willingness to help, their empathic
characteristics, and the fact that they were indigenous to the
neighborhood. In the widow program, however, instead of
choosing people because of race or economic status, we would
use marital status as the critical factor. The outreach would
come from a widowed person who had accommodated to her
own loss and who wanted to help others. Widows would visit
widows, reaching out as neighbors. There would be no stigma
and no question of psychiatric deficiency, for they would come
as friends, neighbors, and fellow sufferers, as did the members
of the existing mutual-help groups (Silverman, 1967). They also
would serve, as Goffman (1963) has described, a bridging function for people in what I later came to realize was a stigmatized
situation (Silverman, 1970).

Based on what I had learned about accommodation, I assumed that the widowed helper typically would have been
widowed for about two years. Since I wanted the widowed
helper to depend on her own experience as a basis for helping, it
would be very difficult for her to work alone. I proposed that
we search for a group of widows to be helpers. A mutual-help
program for widows began to take form.

Although the Widow-to-Widow program was directed by a
professional person and was a part of the Laboratory of Com-

munity Psychiatry of the Department of Psychiatry at Harvard Medical School, it operated as a mutual-help program. As its organizational sponsor, the Laboratory of Community Psychiatry was concerned primarily with demonstrating the feasibility of a new idea. As its professional director, I advised more than directed the Widow-to-Widow program, and I assumed the responsibility for documenting its design, activities, and results. While I have reported elsewhere on some aspects of the program (Silverman, 1966, 1967, 1969b, 1981; Silverman et al., 1974; Silverman & Cooperband, 1975), the pages that follow contain the fullest account.

6　Widow-to-W
Organizatio

Overview

The Widow-to-Widow project read
munity of 250,000 within the city
was chosen because, unlike other pa
nized geographic boundaries and a
religious population. With its death
year, the community offered a suf
reaved (approximately 250 people we
test and evaluate the feasibility of a ne
Our aim was to reach every new wi
offer of help.

The helper would be another widov
her experience to help others, who had
two years, who lived in or near the targe
was able to use her own experience in h
aides were recruited to represent the racia
sition of the community, since at a time c
considered appropriate to be ecumenical.
to be attractive enough that someone would
if she appeared at the door.

A community advisory board made
helped to set policy, legitimate the service
recruit helpers, and decide on the target
initially the project aimed to reach both wido
we found it was practically impossible to re

helpers. Si
reaching o
munity, th
only wido
younger v
already h
under 60

Five
been inv
had beer
would re
bility of
aides, w
without
include
three w
progra
black,

In
death
from t
wome
the hu
would
the d
were
fune
begi
the
to g

the
hov
the
oth
pr
Th
at
th

telephone at home so that she could be available as the widows needed her but without interfering with the regular life of the aide's family. They designed informal note paper, and they composed a letter that they would use for introducing themselves about one month after a death had occurred (Silverman et al., 1975, p. 18). The aides had decided that reaching out any sooner would be meaningless, since the new widow would not yet be able to think of herself as a widow. They questioned the usual concept of six-month recovery or even putting a timetable on accommodation and concluded that it would be at least two years before a widow "would have her head screwed back on and could begin to look ahead."

As project director, my role was to document what they did and to be supportive and helpful as needed. Their life experience gave them an expertise that I did not have, and so the aides would teach me about bereavement and widowhood. We were colleagues in every sense of the word, meeting weekly to review the aides' activities and to document what they were doing. Since the aides were inconsistent about record keeping, these weekly meetings were the main source of data about the intervention the aides developed. This project was an experiment without the traditional guidelines and routines for intervention. We learned as we went along and my task was to document what we learned.

Activities

The first widow served became a widow on May 26, 1967. The aide's introductory note to the new widow included the time of a planned visit and offered the widow the option of calling to cancel the visit or change the time. As aides quickly discovered, some women would call to cancel and then talk for several hours on the telephone. Some women were receptive to the visit, while others preferred to remain telephone confidantes for some time, even as long as a year. Many women would say they had no need but be receptive to having the aide call again. Sometimes, after a year with no further contact, an aide might hear from one of these women: She suddenly was feeling very alone and, experiencing her grief for the first time, was frightened. Other women were simply not at home when the aide visited, but they were pleased when the aide called on the telephone, and in time they accepted an opportunity to meet. Most of the new widows were at home and eager to talk.

The initial one-to-one contact was important. As patterns of similarity in people's problems emerged, small group meetings were planned around such common problems as dependent children at home. Aides sometimes would introduce people to each other when they lived in the same neighborhood. The widows wanted some social contacts, and the aides planned several picnics and backyard cookouts.

Over time, interventions followed the pattern of an initial one-to-one outreach, either on the telephone or in person. Sometimes this would include the aide going to a movie with the widow or spending an evening with her and her family. Eventually, the time would be right to bring her into a small group to talk about common problems, and into social networks and activities. On their own, the widows began to travel together and to develop new friendships that extended beyond the program. Some women became ready to serve as helpers themselves and did so informally. Their patterns of response to intervention reflected their changing needs as they moved through the stages of transition.

Many of these women later joined the Widowed Service Line (Abrahams, 1972), which developed out of the original Widow-to-Widow program. Staffed by volunteer widows and widowers, it served the Greater Boston area and was intended to supplement an outreach program like Widow-to-Widow or to serve as an alternative way of reaching a greater number of both widows and widowers. Three aides from the Widow-to-Widow program coordinated the project, training and supervising the volunteers. Some volunteers were widows who had been helped by the original program, and others were active in local social clubs. A telephone answering service was used for incoming calls. Messages were picked up two to three times a day, and each volunteer spent an evening a week returning the calls and then remained involved with the callers as needed. Every call was returned within 24 hours. If the director thought that there was an emergency, she called herself. The line was advertised in local newspapers and in special community service announcements on television and radio.

When the original Widow-to-Widow project ended in 1971, the widow aide who was Jewish joined a storefront program sponsored by the Jewish Welfare Federation. Her goal was to see how a Widow-to-Widow program would work with elderly women and as part of a regular service program in a community action agency. She identified new widows from death certificates of men over 50 years old and sent them introductory notes on agency stationery. She then involved the widows in ongoing social programs of the agency and in other service programs as needed.

The Widowed Population

The original Widow-to-Widow program reached out to 430 widows over a period of two and a half years. The analysis of data, however, was based on only the first 300, so that all the women included in the analysis would be women who had been widows for at least a year. Of the first 300, 67 are not included in the analysis for various reasons: Several died before the widow could connect with the project, others had moved, and still others had been separated many years from the deceased and did not consider themselves this man's widow. The analysis of data therefore reflects 233 women who had been widowed for at least one year.[1]

Over the year and a half of Widow-to-Widow outreach in the Jewish community, 99 women were widowed and eligible for the project's help. Of these, two women died within two

---

[1]Data were gathered from death certificates, from interviews with the widow's aides, from staff meeting notes, and from meetings with the widows in groups. In addition, 35 of the women who had accepted involvement in the project were interviewed in depth at least one year after their involvement, and an additional 19 women who had dependent children were interviewed three years after their husband's death. The project also made a follow-up contact with every widow who refused the project's help, and 35 of them agreed to be interviewed in depth.

weeks of their husbands, two were divorced, and two moved, so that the analysis is based on the 93 widows actually contacted. Most of these women were indeed elderly, judging from their husbands' ages: 9 of the husbands were between 50 and 59, 31 were between 60 and 69, 39 were between 70 and 79, and 14 were over 80.

Most of the widows' husbands died between ages 51 and 60 (42%) and between 61 and 65 (32.9%). The rest were younger men, between 41 and 50 (15.6%) or under 40 (9.5%). At the time of their husbands' deaths, most of the widows were full-time housewives (60%); those who worked were secretaries, salespeople, or factory workers. Only nine of these 233 women began to work for the first time after their husbands died; most needed Social Security or supplementary wages to survive; and 15 women received assistance from public welfare to supplement their Social Security. Neither race nor religion influenced the response rate. Reflecting the community as a whole, most of the women reached were white (92.2%) and the rest were black. Most of the white women were Catholic (52%), 17.5 percent were Protestant, and 13.5 percent were Jewish.

Most women were still concerned with child rearing (60%), and of those who had children at home, the majority (72%) still had children aged 16 or under to care for. A third of the widows either had no children or no children living at home, and of these women most lived alone, though several had aged parents or widowed siblings in the house.

Almost all the widows were embedded in extended family networks that they saw as supportive and willing to be helpful, but three reported that they had no family available. For the most part, they had grown children, siblings, and parents in the neighborhood nearby. Many had physicians or clergy they turned to for help. The vast majority of widows reported that with time the help available from these networks declined. Although they still could count on their family and still went to their physicians, the help became less relevant and less helpful than it had been initially.

In summary, these widows were typical of the general population in this community and what you would expect to find in any widowed population. The widows were mostly middle aged, still concerned with child rearing, involved in extended family networks, and living in the community where they were born and raised. The need for additional support at the time of their husbands' deaths might not be immediately evident, yet 60 percent of these widows accepted the aides' offers of help and 28 percent of those who had refused said later they would have accepted had they understood more about what the program offered.

The program for elderly Jewish widows had the same response rate. Most of their children had moved on to more middle-class communities, as would many of the widows who could afford to. Family for the most part were still nearby in the small geographic area of Greater Boston.

In the first seven months that the Widowed Service Line was in existence, 750 people called, 90 percent of whom were women. Callers ranged in age from 24 to 90. The modal age was 51 to 60, with 36 percent in this group; 30 percent were over 60 years of age, 22 percent were 41 to 50, and 12 percent were under 40.

The Outreach Service Model

The service goal of the Widow-to-Widow project was to facilitate the widow's transition as she changed from the role of wife to the role of widow to the role of a formerly married woman. The content of the help also would change as the widow moved from one stage of her transition to another. A unifying theme was learning. Widows needed to learn about the changes they faced and how to deal with them, and the aides were the teachers. Since this type of helping had not been done before, the aides were learning as well.

The Mutual-Help Relationship

Since widowed people typically do not know—just as professional people have not recognized—that bereavement initiates a process of change, a guiding premise was to reach out and meet the new widows wherever they were. What a widowed aide could do better than anyone else in this regard was to create an optimal atmosphere for learning. From the outset, the new widow found it easier to talk with someone who understood. She could share her feelings and concerns and hear the aide reflect back her own past—but similar—experiences. The new widow felt legitimated, less alone with her feelings and difficulties. Over and over again, the new widows expressed relief at finding someone who could really understand what they felt. Their feelings became normal and surmountable. The aide was a friend and confidante, offering support and encouragement.

Some women had had poor marriages and felt guilty as they began to redirect their lives while experiencing relief or pleasure that they were no longer burdened by their marital relationship. The aide could understand this feeling. She could reassure the widow that a woman could be glad as well as bereft, that she did not need to feel guilty about the pleasure she and her children were now getting out of their lives.

The aide also had information for dealing with practical realities that a woman alone confronts. When the widow was ready, the aide helped her to build a bridge back to the real world. She had firsthand experience and knowledge about finding a job, locating financial counseling, getting benefits, and arranging programs for the children. The aide herself had once had to "repeople her life." Above all, she could help the new widow learn how to be a single woman, how to live alone, and how to see hope for a satisfying future. In a sense, the aides taught the new widows the "tricks of the trade" (Goffman, 1963).

The project intentionally stayed open in its concept of how widows and aides would relate, the roles they would play, and the relationships they could have under the project's auspices. The aides were always available, on call day or night, and help was not scheduled. Help also was not limited in form: It began one-on-one, but when a person was ready it could include groups, networking, referrals, ad hoc meetings, picnics, and so forth. The aide–widow relationship also was open. When one aide could not offer the widow what she needed, the aide introduced her to another aide or to another widow.

The helping relationship was not precious or exclusive. Thus, when women felt it was important to them to be needed and to help others, the aides pointed to outside volunteer activities or to becoming helpers inside the project, both in the outreach program and in the Widowed Service Line (Silverman, 1972). A widow in the program did not have to remain in the role of recipient to stay involved. She could aspire to be a helper, and, as in any friendship, she could reciprocate. Many widows became volunteer helpers to other widows they met in the Widow-to-Widow program, and some volunteered for the Widowed Service Line. The program was in effect generating the next generation of helpers.

The widow's ability to accept help that was focused on change seemed related to her ability to accept herself as a widow, at least on an intellectual level. The mutual-help experience seemed to make this easier, and the outreach feature also probably was helpful. When a woman who is a role model invites you to participate and you see that she is attractive, functioning with enough energy to reach out, and apparently finding satisfaction and pleasure in her new life, it is less frightening to call yourself a widow (Silverman, 1978, 1981).

The Widow-to-Widow program aides did get paid, but they did not see themselves as professionals. They developed their own helping styles based on their own experiences and personalities; some developed an objectivity that seemed close to a professional's way of conceptualizing the helping role. Abrahams (1976) looked at the helping styles of the aides and discovered a range in their degree of personal involvement and how much they brought the new widow into their own lives. Their different styles could be complementary in this setting. They worked as a team, helping each other, teaching each other how to be helpful in particular instances, and served as monitors for each other when they felt they were getting too involved to be helpful. For example, one widow wanted to borrow money from an aide. The other aides helped the aide to see why this was not a good idea; this particular widow was a spendthrift and needed to learn some of the facts of life with regard to money management.

From the experience of the aide in the Jewish community

agency, the project learned that an aide working alone feels isolated. Trained agency staff tended to look down on her and wanted to supervise her to ensure "quality" service. This of course was antithetical to the work she was doing. Since the professionals did not value experiential knowledge, she needed the support of peers who could appreciate what she was doing.

The Project Director Role

The aides used me as a consultant to give them permission and perspective. Some widows were complaining and frightened as they grappled with the need to change their lives. The process of growth could be slow and laborious. Somewhat outside, I could see progress and could reflect this back for the aide.

As a consultant, I also helped the aides to learn enough about agencies and professional practice that they could be helpful to the widows in their dealings with agencies. As in the real world, the widows were involved in many helping relationships. The relationship with the aide was never seen as conflicting with professional help. The widow was in charge of deciding how many helpers she needed. With time, some widows who had mentally ill adult children who abused them shared their dilemmas with the aide. They had needed help all along in separating from the troubled son or daughter, but had feared the aide would reject them as many of their friends had done. They were embedded in professional helping networks that were not always effective in helping with real problems.

Relating to Other Agencies

When the focus of help was on issues of widowhood, the aide could help even the most troubled women. In several instances, especially where a widow had children, widows went or were referred to a family agency or a mental health clinic. Serving in a liaison role, the aide found herself educating the clinicians about bereavement issues that the family was facing. Agencies could not always respond to a psychiatric emergency, and it was often the aide who held a family's hand over the weekend. When one daughter threatened suicide, it was the aide who talked to her and quieted her down until the agency (which advertised an "emergency" service) could see her. Hospitalization, the alternative, did not seem appropriate. Eventually, with someone mediating the tension between mother and daughter, the situation eased. Sometimes, the aide interpreted agency help to a family, and only with this support did they stay long enough to learn for themselves that the agency could be helpful.

The meaning of outreach should be understood better. People were grateful to the aide for not requiring them to decide that they needed help or what kind they needed. They did not think of their interactions with aides as receiving "help" or as reflections of their need or inadequacies; aides were seen as friends guiding friends. The focus was not on problems but on people needing other people. Opening its door all the way, a real outreach program opens itself to the full range of lifestyles and problems in the community. The Widow-to-Widow aides learned how to evaluate what they found, how to make people feel comfortable, and how to keep the focus on learning to cope with grief.

III

Findings of the Widow-to-Widow Project

7 Overview of Findings

The chapters in this part examine the characteristics, needs, and experiences of widows who accepted and those who refused the help of the Widow-to-Widow program. This chapter summarizes these findings and also reports on the users of the Widowed Service Line. The next chapters deal in greater detail with several major themes that appeared to be associated both with the widows' responses to the offer of help and with such factors as the ages of children, preexisting psychological problems, and employment status.

Since the Widow-to-Widow project was an intervention that aimed to have an impact on women's responses to their widowhood, one might reasonably ask whether the project made any difference in those responses. This question is discussed in the closing chapter of the book. Important as this question is, the broader contribution of the intervention program was the insight it gave into how an unselected population of women coped with widowhood. The widows in this program were not a select group who felt a need for assistance and sought it out. The program reached out to whole populations within a given community. The initial program reached out to every newly widowed woman whose husband was under the age of 65 when he died. In the later phase of the program, outreach extended to widows whose husbands were over 50. Consequently, the program reached families with a wide range of experience with problems. Some had serious and long-standing financial, physical, or emotional problems; were accus-

83

tomed to asking for help; and had established relationships with
social agencies, public welfare, or psychiatric clinics. Most, however, had never before had any contact with an agency or
received assistance from anyone outside the family. Thus, the
findings reflect an unusually broad picture of widowhood, the
kinds of assistance that women may need during this time, and
what an aide can do to help (see Part IV).

Widows Who Accepted Help

The aide was available in a flexible, informal manner over the
first year of each new widow's bereavement. This gave the
widow time to consider her changing needs and to decide if and
when she wanted to meet the aide or spend time talking on the
phone.

To reiterate, widows who accepted help became involved
in the program at various times and in different ways. Some
would only talk on the phone with the aide, and some waited for
six or eight months before meeting the aide for the first time at a
meeting or social gathering. Some women said initially that they
had no need for help and then called back a year later; knowing
they had a resource to turn to, they became involved as they
became aware of their needs. Many others responded readily to
the idea of a visit from the aide as suggested in the aide's
introductory letter.

Profiles

Nearly two-thirds of the 233 women in the sample analyzed,
that is, 145 women, accepted the offer of help. (The elderly
Jewish women who became involved in a later phase of the
program were not part of this sample.) Among those women
whose husbands had been ill for an extended period of time, the
percentage who eventually accepted was even higher, at 75 percent. In addition, two demographic variables were statistically
related to accepting the offer of help. First, as might be expected, women who did not work were more likely to accept
help than those who did work, regardless of age, religion, or

socioeconomic status. Second, when employment status was disregarded, the most significant factor was whether or not the woman had dependent children at home. Widowed mothers were the most likely of all the widows to accept help when it was first extended.

The numbers of these younger widowed mothers accepting help were disproportionate to the numbers of such women in the widowed population as a whole. They did not complain particularly about the problems with their children, but they seemed to experience their widowhood with a greater urgency than did other widows. These findings are consistent with the findings of self-referral programs (Parkes, 1977; Raphael, 1977; Barrett, 1978).

Of the older widows in the Jewish group (those whose husbands were 65 years of age or older), 75 percent accepted the offer of help. By the time this program was initiated, however, the basic program had been established in the community, which may account for the higher positive response. Two-thirds of these women lived alone, but this did not seem to make a difference in their accepting the aide's offer to visit.

Like their younger counterparts, older widows who worked were less likely to accept help. What also did matter, and was clearly not due to chance differences, was the existence of nearby family whom the widows experienced as helpful. In this regard, the older women were like the younger ones: fewer of the women who accepted had family nearby. Family consisted of children and siblings with whom the widow had regular contact. One widow's sister had been helped earlier in the program, and this sister was now helping her "as she had been helped." Over time, the families' interest was not sustained and the help was not as meaningful. These women then sought help. Interestingly, women who went to live with their children responded to the aide's offer with great eagerness. Once they moved, they felt isolated and lonely living in new neighborhoods where their only connection to the community was through their children. Studies since have demonstrated that women who reject the grandmother role and who remain actively involved with peers have a better adjustment than those who do not (Arling, 1976).

Needs

In only a few instances did a widow respond to the offer of help
by indicating that she was in a panic. In one such instance, once
the widow knew help was available, she allowed herself to
experience the full intensity of her anxiety. This was an unchar-
acteristic response for her, and she was able to pull herself
together with the friendship and support of the aide. One
woman who had no family except a nephew in a distant city saw
the aide's arrival as "a piece of heaven dropping into my living
room."

Almost all (81%) of those who wanted help accepted because they needed to talk with another widow who would
understand their feelings. Although they did not always want to
talk about these feelings, they found it helpful to have them
acknowledged and to hear that because they were newly widowed they might have special needs. These women wanted
friendship and companionship; they also wanted information
about how others had managed.

One-third (33%) wanted help with problems related to housing. Some women believed that their neighborhood was becoming dangerous. Others felt that their housing was inadequate,
and some wanted to move to be nearer relatives. One woman
was evicted because of her drinking. This was not the first time
this had happened to her, but now she did not have her husband
as a buffer.

Some (28%) mentioned problems with their children (adult
as well as minor); 25 percent simply needed reassurance that
they would weather the current crisis successfully. Some were
concerned about inadequate income (24%), some specifically
mentioned difficulties with relatives or family who did not
understand their current situation (23%), some wanted advice
about or support in getting a job or going back to school (22%),
and some wanted specific financial advice such as with benefit
claims (19%). Several families immediately asked the aide for
clothes or money, to intervene with welfare, and so forth. Such
requests seemed to be almost reflexive responses, as the widows
saw a new resource in the aide. They were accustomed to going

to agencies for this kind of help, and their needs became more critical in the husband's absence.

In this population were four women with a history of alcoholism and four women with histories of schizophrenia or severe depressive illness. They were between the ages of 35 and 60; some had grown children, and others were still caring for young children at home. The problems of the women who drank clearly were related to the drinking, which was immediately apparent to everyone but themselves. The other emotional problems became apparent to the aide only over time.

Among the older women in the Jewish group, widows sought help with housing, getting medical attention, getting to and from doctors' appointments, and with loneliness.

Widows Who Refused Help

Women who were considered to have refused help were those who never became involved in any way during the active period of the project. Of the 233 contacted and included in this analysis, 91 women (39%) refused the offer of help. Women gave the following reasons for refusing, in descending order of frequency: (1) too busy with job, family, or setting affairs in order; (2) plenty of support from family and friends; (3) grown children refuse to allow the aide to talk with their mother; and (4) independent and no need for support. In some instances the aide could never make contact; other women would not open the door; a small number of women at first responded favorably on the phone and subsequently refused any contact.

In one frustrating situation, the widow continually said she had no need and refused to see the aide, while the widow's 18-year-old daughter would tell the aide that she felt very sad without her father and that both she and her mother were crying a lot. The daughter wanted the aide to visit, but the aide could do very little if the widow continually refused. While the first initiative came from the aide, what happened subsequently depended on the new widow, her view of her needs, and her reaction to someone offering to talk and be a friend.

Follow-up interviews with these women between two and three years after they became widows were aimed at learning more about why they had refused and whether they differed in their accommodation from those who accepted. Two widows had remarried and would not agree to be interviewed; 22 in addition to the women who had remarried formally refused; 27 had moved; and five refused by avoiding any contact with the interviewer. Thus, 35 women agreed to a follow-up interview.

Included with those who refused to be interviewed were seven women who had been very friendly to the aide when she first called, encouraged her to call back, and thought it was nice that someone cared. They were rarely at home when the aide called, however, and never accepted any of the aide's invitations. These women worked and were also very involved with their children. We discovered that several had moved out of town to be near their children, and the others did not want to be bothered with an interview. Their method of coping seemed to be to keep very busy and to avoid encounters with the past. We cannot prejudge this as a poor solution. In the end they were counted as people who refused both the aide's offer of help and the follow-up interview.

Another interesting group of people who refused were the nine widows whose children answered for them. In seven of these instances, the children continued to intervene on their mothers' behalf. The children had all called in response to the initial letter to say that they were caring for their mother, that she was busy with her family, and that she had no need. In one instance where the mother started to talk with the aide on the telephone, her daughter called to her mother from the background that since she did not know the caller she should hang up, which the widow quickly did. In trying to locate the woman for a follow-up interview, we learned that she had moved out of the state to be near her son. One daughter was very hostile and told the aide, "Don't bother my mother." The aide learned from a neighbor who was involved in the program that this daughter was divorced from an alcoholic husband and had come home expecting mother to take care of her and her young child after her father died. The widow worked and spent a good deal of time outside of the home because she could not deal with her daughter. The husband/father had been better able to set limits. Three years later this widow and daughter had moved to a house in the suburbs.

The Widowed Service Line

More than half of those who called the Widowed Service Line had heard about it from television. One-fifth read about it in their newspaper. Some church bulletins printed announcements about the line, and a few people learned about it from a friend. As the line became better known, mental health professionals and clergy referred widowed people whom they felt unable to help with their specific problems.

Almost half (46%) of the 750 people who called the Widowed Service Line during the first seven months had been widowed within the last two years and were handling the early problems of grief and disengagement from a previous lifestyle. They were only beginning to engage in new roles and relationships. A smaller proportion (23%) had been widowed for three to six years, and they were still trying to adjust to and develop a new lifestyle. One-third of the callers still had not adjusted after seven years of widowhood.

Callers requested help with a variety of problems. The majority called complaining of their loneliness. Most of these callers wanted to meet people, but 20 percent simply required a listener. One-fifth of the callers asked for specific information about such things as financial assistance, budgeting, employment or training, housing, legal matters, health facilities, professional care for themselves or their children, and so forth. For most of the callers, financial problems were not major issues. While many of them lived on an adequate or tight budget, many (45%) did not say a word about their financial situation. Many callers were given additional information about financial benefits, although this was not the problem about which they called. To reach low-income, minority populations, an outreach program may be more appropriate.

The three main categories of callers' needs—for a listener, to meet people, and for specific practical information—seemed to be significantly related to the stage of widowhood. Widowed people who called within the first year of bereavement were most likely to need an understanding listener. During the impact or recoil periods, they were beginning to experience the full impact of the loss, and they needed to talk about this with someone who could understand. Callers who were widowed from approximately two to six years were most likely to be struggling to move toward an accommodation to their widowhood. They were trying out new roles, developing new relationships, and looking for ways to reengage in the social system. They asked how to make new contacts and where to go to meet new people. Callers who had been widowed a longer time (seven years or more) also requested information about meeting people, but a greater proportion of these people had specific requests about financial, legal, housing, and employment problems.

These calls for help suggest another critical stage for the older widowed person. When their children have grown and left home, they must for the first time face the need to live alone. This same observation pertains to a group of women who refused the offer of help in the Widow-to-Widow program. The widow who depended heavily on work or family for a meaningful self-definition may be in difficulty when the family disperses or when she reaches retirement age. Children leaving home and retirement are always transitions, and they may require different adaptations when a person is a widow or widower.

The people most likely to call were those living alone (49%) and those living with children under the age of 16 (30%). People in these groups, regardless of age, seemed to experience the most immediate pressures after the death of a spouse. Although most of the people who called were not working (61%), those most likely to call for help in making new friends were those who were working. While a job may have alleviated the immediate distress of bereavement, it was no substitute for the intimacy of friendship.

In response to volunteers' questions about social life, 61 percent said they felt very isolated, 17 percent were too newly bereaved to consider the questions, and only 22 percent felt they had an active social life. For 46 percent, relatives played an important role in helping during the initial period of bereavement. Most families, though, are not helpful over the long run, as widows' needs change. For example, most callers who were helped to make new friends and had a satisfactory social life received this help from friends (43%) or from joining a widowed persons' club (34%). Perhaps those widowed people whose families can meet their changing needs or who have friends who are helpful do not reach out for additional assistance. This possibility is consistent with the findings regarding those who refused offers of help from the Widow-to-Widow program. Either there were other widows in the family or the widow had friends who were widowed.

The service line afforded an easy opportunity to put people in touch with each other. For example, two women called who were newly widowed and pregnant, and another young widow who called the line told the volunteer that her baby had been born after her husband died. The volunteer arranged for the women to meet, and they formed an informal support group. Others with less dramatic stories were introduced to each other on the telephone so that they could simply share their loneliness with each other and so they might eventually make new friends with whom to visit or go out. The line also enabled people to exchange services. Some women offered child-care services, others wanted to share a house, and several men exchanged repairing something in the house for a home-cooked meal. Some of the women wanted to talk with someone who could guide them in such decisions as buying a car. The volunteer simply would put these people in touch with each other.

Volunteers rarely gave their home numbers to a caller. It was the volunteer who followed up and kept in touch with the caller. If the caller wanted to reach a particular volunteer, they did so through the answering service. The volunteers felt that most of their callers could be served adequately in two or three telephone conversations. The stage of unloading feelings and getting into the deeper feelings associated with the callers' problems usually could be reached in the first or second conversation. One or two supportive calls were often sufficient to help the caller over a bad spell or to give him or her the necessary push to start getting involved with new friends and activities.

The line received several calls from people with very serious emotional problems. Several were drinking excessively, as
was apparent from the first call. If they were willing to acknowledge that they were drinking, they were referred to AA or
another program for drinking problems. Most of the people
with serious problems were already involved in other helping
programs. For example, the widowed director of the program
returned the call of a woman who told the answering service she
wanted to kill herself. The call extended late into the night as
this woman bemoaned the fact that no one listened to her, not
her children and not even her psychiatrist whom she had seen
that morning. Each time that we received calls like this, we
found that the caller had an active network of helpers. We
cannot assume that the existing networks were unable to listen
and hear the special needs related to widowhood, since these
callers also did not make good use of their contact with a widow
who "did understand." For these people, nothing seemed to
change, and they continued to complain. They had profound
problems beyond the scope of this type of service, and they
were already actively engaged in a helping network. If no
network existed, the volunteer's role was to engage them in an
appropriate helping relationship.

The line also had silent consumers. We know that the adver-
tisements were read by many more people than those who
actually called. A widow I met socially several years later told
me that she kept the phone number by her bed. She never
called, but she found it comforting to know that someone was
there. By its very existence, then, the line was helpful. It must be
assumed that this woman was not unique in the way she used the
service. She and others like her remain the silent consumers.

8 Widows Who Accepted Help

Widows with Young, Dependent Children

Widows with dependent children were decidedly more likely than others to want to see the aide as soon after the death as possible. They were eager to talk to someone: "The children are good but it's not like talking to a grownup." While other widows deferred the visit, talked at length on the phone, or were simply not at home for the initial visit, this was not true of women with young children. Out of 45 who had children under the age of 16, 41 accepted. Widowed mothers talked about the special difficulty that having children created. Almost immediately they had to confront the reality of their loss. Unlike their peers whose children were grown, they could not run from the house or their daily routines or responsibilities. Every day they had to face the reminders that their husbands were dead.

Children were open about their grief, and many widows had difficulty with this. One woman compared her children's questions to "a knife being stuck in my throat." At the same time, they did not want to burden their children with their own grief, and they would withdraw, inadvertently causing the children to lose both parents. Many found they could not sustain their maternal roles consistently, and they were concerned about their ability to discipline the children. They found that they had to be better organized than they were before in order to respond to their children's needs as well as to their own often-immobilizing feelings. These mothers often were confused by the children's behavior and wondered what could be associated with grief and what would be typical behavior at a particular age.

The youngest widow in this population was 19 years old and had a one-year-old child; the oldest was in her late 50s and had a 12-year-old child at home. These widows usually had several children at home. The help they wanted focused on the depth of their children's reactions and their own lack of preparation for single parenthood.

The following is a report of a study of 19 of these families. They had 56 children among them. From this account we begin to get a sense of why the widow with dependent children at home responded so readily to the offer of friendship from another widow. The material shows how children reacted to their fathers' deaths and how their widowed mothers tried to understand and respond to their children. The needs of the children could not wait while the widow dealt with her own grief, yet her own grief interfered with her ability to be aware of their needs and at times prevented her from responding appropriately.

Dealing with the Event

Most often the widow would not remember how she had told her children that their father was dead. The period around the death was a blur. Widows would talk about their children's reactions but did not understand the meaning of these reactions. Most of the children seemed not to believe what they were told or tried to deny it, and the way they handled this was appropriate to their age. For example, a 10-year-old child beat on the older sister who told him the news when he came home from school, while a three-year-old child asked when Daddy was coming back. Widows often interpreted the child's denial or sense of shock as meaning that they did not understand or appreciate what had happened. Nonetheless, widows often used phrases like "they were crushed," "he became very quiet," "he couldn't sleep nights," and "they were heartbroken." They could not face the fact that their children might be grieving. To face the child's grief might mean one more thing to which they would have to respond. They wanted to believe that the children were fine, and they kept looking for reassuring signs that this was so.

To see a child break down and cry was more than they could manage, and this was a primary reason that widows did not take younger children to the funeral. They wanted to avoid the children becoming unnecessarily upset and breaking down and crying. One mother, recalling her own fear as an adolescent at her mother's funeral, did not take her six-year-old daughter to the funeral. Another arranged a signal with her adolescent son to remind each other not to cry at the funeral. The most vivid thing one mother remembered about the funeral was that her 18-year-old daughter would not look into the coffin because she wanted to remember her father as he was. Even a year later, another widow was sorry she had taken her 11 year old to the anniversary mass. He became so upset that he could not stop crying, and she could see no positive value in this expression of feelings.

Hiding One's Feelings

One characteristic of these widows was their reluctance to lose control and to express the strong feelings they were experiencing. Although they did not deny the feelings, they did not want to express feelings that they did not know how to manage. They were struggling with their own acceptance of the new reality, and their children's questions and needs made their own pain more profound. These widowed mothers developed a pattern of avoiding discussions about their husbands, and this kept them from dealing directly with the children's feelings. The widows rationalized that the children would be unduly upset by seeing their grief, and they tried to keep themselves from crying in front of the children. One woman acknowledged that this approach made her feel more lonely, but she also claimed, "You can't go around mourning in front of grown boys."

The children responded to their mother's lead. When one boy found his father's driver's license two years after the death, he started to cry and left the room. In another family, the widow reported that her daughters stopped talking about their father when they saw how upset she became. This same widow was upset that her 13-year-old son had become very quiet since his father died and never even brought up his name. Only when it was pointed out to her did she realize that her son's silence was his obedient response to her message.

Most widows found that avoidance did not work over the long run and were grateful for the intervention that interrupted this pattern:

> I tried to keep my feelings from them. A friend, a priest, told me not to and so did Dorothy [the aide]. In the end I let them see my sadness and crying. Now we each share our feelings more honestly. It has brought us closer together.

Children can misunderstand a widowed mother's silence and think that she does not miss their father or care about him:

> I was shocked to discover that they thought I didn't care. This came out when I was talking to my seven-year-old son's teacher. He had managed to explain to her how he felt. I had to force myself to talk about their father and to help them keep their very good memories of him. I don't want them to ever forget their father, but I guess that's what they thought I wanted when I didn't show my feelings.

Understanding the Child's Reactions

Several younger children had sleepless nights and wet their beds for a brief period. One six-year-old boy who became enuretic talked a great deal about his father who had been killed in an automobile accident. He played out crash scenes with his cars for several months. Fortunately he had a sympathetic teacher who encouraged him to talk about the loss, and this made a difference in his behavior at home. His mother had not immediately connected his bedwetting with his reaction to his father's death.

Widowed mothers did not generally recognize that a child might develop difficulty in school or that the school should even be informed about the father's death. Most often the teacher learned from the child what had happened. Some teachers tried to be supportive and listen to the child. In one instance, the teacher called the mother of an 11-year-old boy who told her that he was the man in his family now. She talked over his behavior and linked it to the death and to the way the family was reacting. Another teacher called when she noticed a first-grader's unusual quiet and sadness. These teachers taught the mothers something about helping their children. Teachers are not uniformly supportive, however: a 16-year-old girl reported being told by her teacher two weeks after her father had died that she could not expect any special consideration on this account and must keep up her work or be penalized.

Some children's reactions were more obvious than others. For example, one adolescent reacted with a dramatic renunciation of childhood:

> Her room had been plastered with pictures of the Beatles. The day her father died she went upstairs and took them down. She said, "I'm not a baby any more." I tried to explain to her that she was still a child even if her father had died. But I guess when you go through something like that you never feel the same. The pictures never went back up.

In a sense the child seems to grow up over night. In a subsequent study of bereaved college-aged women, I found a similar pattern of reactions. These young women reported becoming impatient with some of the "frivolous" concerns of their peers and feeling older and out of step with people who had once been close friends.

Based on widows' accounts, children seemed to react in three different ways to their mothers and their families. Some children became terrified that they would lose the surviving parent. Some assumed special responsibilities in the family, in taking care of others. Still others rebelled against the family, withdrew socially, and began slipping in schoolwork. This latter group caused their mothers the most concern, often with cause.

In a family with several children, the one child who would have such an extreme reaction tended to be a boy between the ages of 14 and 19, although two teenaged girls also had such reactions.

How two or three of these several reactions might intertwine with each other in a single child is a question beyond the limits of the data, but I have no reason to believe that the three types of responses are mutually exclusive. The responsible child also could be the frightened child, for example:

> I don't know how I took care of the babies that year. I relied on my six-year-old to help. This forced her to be mature and more self-reliant. If I needed to run out to the store for a minute I had to let her watch the babies. About 10 months after my husband died she had a dream that I was lying on the couch making noises. She got pills which did not help. I tried to reassure her that I wasn't going anywhere.

The Child Who Is Afraid.   The child's fear of losing a surviving parent takes many forms. One woman said that her youngest, age eight, had nightmares shortly after her father died, but the widow had not been certain the dreams were connected to his death:

> She had a dream about me being taken away from her, or she couldn't find her way home, or it always seemed as if she found herself alone at the end of the dream or nightmare.

She came to realize the connection and also eventually understood why her middle daughter, age 10, would not let her mother leave the house unless she knew where she was going, who was driving, and when she would be home:

> If I came home five minutes late she was a nervous wreck. I guess that's how it affected them, not in the usual way with the tears and crying and the grief you naturally expect.

Without interpreting or understanding the behavior as a reaction to the death, she had responded by being there when they needed her.

Like most widowed mothers, this widow had expected the children's grief to be expressed directly in tears and sadness, and she therefore did not connect the children's other unusual behavior with grieving. Until they could see the link, some women were reluctant to indulge their children because they feared spoiling them, or they were worried that, with father gone, the children would think they could get away with things.

One 12-year-old boy, whose father had been murdered in his front hall, refused to go back and forth to school unless escorted by his mother. His mother recognized his real fear of the neighborhood but also saw that his clinging was a result of his fear of losing her. It took her a while to realize that having these fears was "no sin." In another case, a six-year-old only child expressed her fear of losing her mother by insisting that she walk her home from school every day.

One widow recalled that her children were paralyzed by seeing her cry on the anniversary of their father's death. Perhaps children do not want their mother to cry in front of them because they understand that they also can lose their mother to her grief. A younger child, who was perhaps more ingenuous and less fearful of saying what he thought, asked directly, "Who will take care of me if something happens to you?"

Children in this group were generally small children, and mothers actively sought guidance with the children's problems and their management. Above all, these mothers felt acutely the special loneliness that comes from trying to care for little children alone. While they worried about what was best for their children, what was most unbearable were the long evening hours after the children had gone to bed and the house had become empty. They needed to share their isolation and despair.

The Responsible Child. The assumption of additional responsibility is a more subtle phenomenon to assess and describe. It can be seen in a 12-year-old girl's admonition to her mother, "Don't cry while we are at school." The concern can be shared among several children:

> They didn't want to go to school at first. They worried about me at home alone. When I insisted they go, I think they were glad to get

out of the house. They also said that my middle girl, who is closest
to me, would always stay by me so I didn't have to be alone when
they grew up.

Older children, especially the girls, also could be protective of
and helpful to the widow:

They try to get me out, over my depression. I'd be lost without
them. They protect and baby me from all the sadness I feel. I
almost had a breakdown after my husband died. Working helped
me, too. Everyone there worked at keeping me busy and occupied.

One woman said her older girls "became women, and they were
very brave and very helpful." She thought it must be very hard
for a woman with no older children. Another woman who had
agreed with her son not to cry at the funeral saw him as "a
charm":

He's never been anything but courage and encouragement to me.
If he cried, which he did with his older brother and sister, he never
let me see it.

This pattern of behavior did not give the widows much
trouble, and the children seemed to do well. Most of the girls
mentioned went on to finish school, and some went away to
college. The children did not seem to be overwhelmed by what
they gave their mothers, in part because these were reciprocal
relationships. Their mothers were able to reassure them that
they would take care of them, would continue mothering them,
and would consider their needs.

The Withdrawn and Troubled Child. Widowed mothers
were at a loss to understand or to know how to respond to those
children who withdrew, began doing poorly in school, and
seemed to lose their purpose and direction. These children
tended to be boys, usually from 9 to 14 years old. In all, five
children from five families showed this pattern. With one exception, the fathers had been very much involved with their families. Some were considered gentle, leaving discipline and the

like to their wives; others were the disciplinarians and pacesetters for the family. Their relationships with their wives seemed to be good as well. The exception was a man who was a compulsive gambler and whose wife had threatened divorce. All five of the troubled children were youngest or middle children with older sisters and had enjoyed special relationships with their fathers.

One of the children was an adolescent girl who at first withdrew completely from school and then from all activities outside of the house. Her brothers fared better:

> They had a rough time. One was his father's alter ego. They had a sense of responsibility and kept going. My daughter just stopped living.

The girl told her mother, "I am closer to Daddy than you are." This girl had spent much of her free time caring for her terminally ill father at home while her mother was working.

One child went so far as to ask his mother, "Why couldn't it have been you instead of Daddy?" In one case, a son's withdrawal occurred immediately after his father's death, but it was a transitory symptom based on his relationship with his mother:

> He's the only man in the house. He must feel picked on. His father used to protect him from me. I was the firm disciplinarian.

Several of the mothers talked about their sons' need for discipline and how a boy needs a father. "If his father was alive, he would have made him work. He was more scared of his father." Although the role of father seemed to them to involve a police function, they saw it as more centrally related to getting the boys to perform properly.

The underlying problem for these sons and their mothers was not that the children needed the control that fathers might symbolize but that the children's role in the family vis-à-vis their mothers was made problematic by the loss of their fathers. These mothers usually had a special relationship with their other

children (often girls), and they closed out the boys. With the
father gone, the boy had in a sense lost both parents. The boy
seemed unable to get close to his mother; indeed, he had always
looked to his father to help him break away from the dependency relationship with his mother, to show him how to link
himself to the outside world, and to be a separate individual.
With father gone, he felt helpless to complete these developmental tasks alone. His solution was to withdraw and to involve
his mother in a more extensive caregiving role than she normally
would have given to a son of his age.

Some of these boys wanted to assume the role of father,
which could have been one way of keeping him around. An only
son had been told directly by relatives that this was expected of
him. Another boy who had been his father's favorite realized
that he was now just like the rest and talked about assuming his
father's place, giving orders and being waited on by the women
in the family. He gave this up when he saw that his mother
would not allow him to behave in this way. When the widowed
mother realized what was happening and made it clear that the
boy was not to assume this responsibility, the problem disappeared. But when the mother had no idea what was going on,
was getting a good deal from the other children, and in fact was
encouraging her son to be like his father, this problem of course
continued. If the child was not having trouble, though, this
assumption of father's role was not a problem:

> My oldest boy takes on more responsibility. He has absorbed his
> father's goodness. He is always asking me if I am all right and if I
> am happy.

Another child's idealizing of his father was less successful—
for himself and the family.

> He idealizes him. He still talks about the way his father punished
> him as better than the ways his friends' fathers treat their children
> now. He really worries me. I think some of his answering back is
> adolescence, but he is becoming a loner, he won't go to Scouts
> anymore, and he's withdrawn and talks about wanting to be an
> artist.

A child's fixation on the father and a simultaneous withdrawal from activities and performance that the father would value can be perplexing:

> He is very emotional. He drives and every once in a while he goes to visit his father's grave. He talks a lot about his father. I keep saying to him, "You'd better grow up and be like your father," and he says, "I will, Ma." He's not like his father, though. My husband was so quiet, but in sports they were alike. But his grades have gone down. He's stopped paying attention. He seems to live in a world of his own.

This pattern of withdrawal and becoming ineffectual seems related to the child's position in the family (usually the only surviving male) and to the way his mother does her mothering when she is bereaved. At this time she sees the children as giving her purpose and meaning and helping her to keep going. She is not fully sensitive to the special care they may need now that their father is gone. For his part, the child may still need his father to help him move away from mother and to teach him how to function independently outside the home. His withdrawn behavior indicates his feeling of helplessness and his ineffectuality in the face of his conflict. His mother's behavior does seem to make a difference in what happens in the long run. As she becomes aware and is able to respond to his special needs, he seems to do better (Silverman & Silverman, 1979).

Only one mother in this group sought professional psychiatric guidance for her child's problem. None of these mothers talked easily about their feelings, and they found it difficult to allow a new person (such as the aide) into their lives. They already had the assistance of friends and family, and they were fearful that they would lose their independence by engaging in a new relationship. They ranged in awareness from an acceptance of their interdependency with others to a denial of any need for such intimacy and a refusal to ever really talk about themselves.

These women were obviously not seriously damaged people from a psychological point of view. Many of them did benefit from and enjoyed involvement in the outreach program.

What is striking about them, though, is that they rarely talked about or confronted these troubled children as problems. Some women needed someone else to point out their children's difficulty. Even then, they might not do anything about it. Rather, most would normalize the difficulty by attributing part of it to adolescence (which cannot be discounted).

Several of these mothers did nothing but worry, but they seemed unable to confront the real issues. One mother, who never really felt in charge of her situation, felt that several teachers in a private school had failed her son by not talking with him or her about his difficulties. Feeling quietly overwhelmed by the whole thing, she finally took someone else's suggestion and put him in another school. She herself never really talked with her son about what could be causing his current problems, just as she had never initiated any conversation with him about his father.

Summary

Mothers of young, dependent children often did not focus explicitly on their children's behavior as a response to loss, even though the range of behavior they described demonstrates that their children did react. For however brief a time period and regardless of their age, children conveyed their feelings in their own concrete behavioral language. Their mothers often could not respond appropriately, in part because they were unaccustomed to interpreting their children's behavior symbolically. An even more important reason the widow cannot focus on her child's needs may be her inability to deal with some aspects of her own grief. She may clearly communicate, "Don't show me you're upset."

By insulating the child from her own grief, the widow really may be protecting herself. She uses avoidance and denial to protect herself and her children from experiencing the pain of their loss. James Agee's novel *A Death in the Family* vividly captures how the child senses his parent's unwillingness to discuss the death:

When you want to know more—about it (and her eyes become still more vibrant) just ask me, just, just ask me and I'll tell you because you ought to know. "How did he get hurt" Rufus wanted to ask, but he knew by her eyes that she did not mean at all what she said, not now anyway, not this minute, he need not ask; and now he did not want to ask because he too was afraid; he nodded to let her know he understood her. [Agee, 1957, p. 253]

In general, the mothers' inability to deal with their children's needs was a result of preoccupation, not neglect. Two mothers in this group of single-parent households did neglect their children, leaving them with babysitters and older siblings, but this was their typical way of managing. One of these women had abandoned the children to her husband for six months before he died. With his death the children were indeed orphaned, and they lost both parents. In the other family, the father and mother had been separated for three months before he died, and nothing changed for the children when this happened as far as the attention they got from their mother.

All of the widowed mothers felt that their children had given meaning to their lives at a time when they were despairing and hopeless. For some this meaning came from their having to be alert and involved in order to respond to their children's needs. Others found meaning in having someone to lean on, someone who could get them up and out of themselves. Even with young children, these widows may have been getting more than giving.

Over time the widowed mothers and their children found ways to temper their sense of loss. Shortly after the death, one widow said, "We talk about him often, but it is like he is on vacation." Religion helped some to acknowledge the reality of the death and to find an appropriate way of remembering. One young adolescent comforted his mother with the thought that his father was "with Jesus" and with telling her there was no reason for so much sadness. In this sense he used religion to help his mother cope with her grief. Others used it to help themselves. One girl, three years after her father's death, prayed to him every night, asking if he were watching her and if he would be proud of her. In some families, children would go to the cemetery regularly. One adolescent, who previously had given up religion, after his father's death went to Mass each month on the same date as the date of his father's death.

Widows with Older, Dependent Children

Many women in their late fifties were still caring for dependent children. In several cases, this dependency was not related to the children's age but to their prior problems. In one case, the problems were profound mental and physical retardation. Others had taken in adult offspring who were having marital difficulty. Still others had grown children who were not yet married and who still lived at home. With the older women, the acceptance of an offer of help was not related to living alone: The same proportion of women with others at home accepted a visit from the aide as did those who lived alone. Older widows shared the common perception that their families were not as helpful to them as they had expected. Their families did not seem to understand their needs as widows, and they could not share their concerns and feelings with them.

The women whose adult offspring were still dependent on them faced special problems. The widow whose son was re- tarded had an aide who came in daily to help bathe and dress this helpless adult. Neighbors came to exercise him and to babysit so she could go out for a few hours a day. A priest from a local church came to help put him to bed. A social worker was encouraging the widow to place her son in an institution now that her husband was dead. Her husband had been ill for a long time and she had cared for him at home as well. The widow asked the Widow-to-Widow aide for help in advocating that she keep the child at home. Without this dependent son, the wid- ow's life and home would be empty.

In two other families, the children had major mental ill- nesses that involved the widow in a continuing caretaking role. It took the aide a long time to learn what was happening with these women. They were eager to be involved but reluctant to have her visit the home. Both children were paranoid, verbally abusive, neglectful in personal hygiene, and erratic in taking their medication; and they found it difficult to stay in a relationship with a mental health clinic.

In one of these two families, the woman was exhausted from caring for her sick husband before he died and protecting him from their son's abuse. The son was an only child in his late thirties and had been ill for many years. His mother met the aide outside the home. Only much later did the aide learn that this widow was embarrassed by her son's behavior and never had people visit. The widow explains:

> I never know what condition I'll find the house. He's a chain smoker and has burned holes in the furniture. He's there all day and when I walk in he can start yelling verbal abuse at me. He won't take his medicine, he won't see the doctor, he can't work.

In the other family, the woman's husband had died suddenly. He had been better able to set limits for his disturbed daughter, who was the oldest of five and had had her first breakdown six months before her father died. Now the widow, who was ineligible for Social Security, had to think of working for the first time. At the same time, she had to learn how to live with her daughter and how to ask her to participate responsibly in the family. The widow feared her daughter's anger and in order to placate her usually did everything she asked. When this mother was invited to talk to a social worker, she did not find it helpful at first: "She went into my history. I didn't know what good that would do." This widow talked with the aide on the telephone about her daughter but did not agree to meet the aide for almost a year. For these women, in spite of their offsprings' ages, the role of mother was still very active, even though they might have been ready to relinquish the role.

Older Widows Alone

Most of the older women had long since finished with child care. With their husbands' deaths, whether they lived alone or not, the factor that joined them with other women was their widowhood. Three issues concerned these older widows: money, health, and companionship. Women in the population over 70 expressed concern that they would not be able to manage as they got older and more infirm. Although we might expect that women in this generation would be largely dependent on their husbands and would have difficulty managing alone, this proved not to be true. Many of these women were from working-class backgrounds, had raised families, had worked when additional income was needed, and were well able to manage a house alone. Many of the husbands had given their paychecks to these widows. Those who were already working were least likely to see the aide. For those who had never worked, getting a job seemed an overwhelming task.

Most of these older women were in difficult financial situations. If they were under 60 with no dependent children at home, they were ineligible for benefits under their husbands' Social Security. One woman's husband had died six weeks before he was eligible for retirement benefits, and she had no income and no choice but to find work for the first time in more than 25 years.

A woman not quite 60 told her son that she would move closer to where he lived in a neighboring suburb, but not into his house. She had a heart condition and hoped to get disability assistance, but she still could care for herself. Although she was denied benefits, she found a job, through a friend, at a telephone answering service. This paid the rent, and she managed. Another widow was surprised that she could find work:

> I had no idea anyone would hire me, and I had less of an idea about how to apply for a job. I couldn't let my children support me. I needed to hear that other women my age found work. Betty showed me how to read the want ads, and we rehearsed what I would say. I couldn't believe it when the phone company offered me a job. They said I was more reliable!

Most of these widows did not know how to reach out beyond the boundaries of their homes to make new friends. Said one, "I'm really a homebody. I never had much to do with the neighbors. My husband and I did everything together."

Even if they had children with whom they were involved in regular visits or telephone calls, this was not sufficient. They needed the aide to share their grief with, and they wanted help in making friends. Several women recently had retired with the idea of retiring along with their husbands. These women particularly needed help building a social network. Some women discovered that they had become a "fifth wheel." They had not anticipated that their friends who were still married would be uncomfortable with them. Sometimes the children were first to recognize their mother's need to make new friends. One daughter in particular encouraged her mother to remain in touch and to get involved. The mother explains:

> It was my wedding anniversary. I wanted my daughter to take me to the cemetery. She agreed only if I would go to the Widow-to-Widow cookout afterwards. I had been talking to Mary for a long time. She and my daughter had both been telling me I had to get out of the house. Best thing I ever did was go to that cookout. Mary introduced me to several other widows right in my own neighborhood.

Some older women found that their children intruded so that they found it difficult to stay in charge of their lives:

> My daughter decided that the neighborhood was too dangerous. I couldn't go out shopping alone. She packed up my things and moved me to her house. I didn't have the energy to argue. Now I am really lonely. Everyone is out of the house during the day and there is no one to talk to. I'd move back to the old neighborhood in a minute if I could find a place I could afford.

As these examples show, grown children played a variety of roles in the lives of these widows. Some became very protective and assumed a parental role with their surviving parent, sometimes insisting that their mother come to live with them. Some were neglectful, while others seemed to respect the mother's needs for attention as well as for privacy. The grief of these older sons and daughters tended to be ignored. Neither the grown children nor the widow expected that the children's grief should be an issue. The focus was on the widow and her grief. In one family, the married daughter began to have difficulty with transient depression a year after her father died. Eventually she saw that her depression related to her father's death and to the unexpressed feelings she had because of her family's preoccupation with her father's cancer during her adolescence.

One woman's adult children found the open letter from the aide and called the aide to tell her not to come, that they would take care of their mother. Initially the widow went along with this, but gradually she became aware of her own needs:

> I went hunting for the letter. Fortunately my daughter had not thrown it away. I reminded them that they were all going to be moving out and that I had to take care of myself. I was going to talk to this woman and find out what it was all about. As I talked to Dorothy, I realized that there were many things I wanted to talk about and I could not share them with the kids. They didn't understand. At 55 I wasn't old. The children really weren't going to support me, no matter what they promised. I needed to work and Dorothy was very encouraging. Smartest thing I ever did was to make that phone call.

Women who had no children were especially lonely, and the aide's visit was important to them. Most of these women had had satisfying marriages. They had nieces and nephews who were like children to them, and they were close to their own sisters and brothers. One holocaust survivor talked endlessly to the aide about her husband and what a poor relationship she had had with him. She complained bitterly about how the neighbors did nothing to help. Her own anger served to isolate her further from people. Finally she moved to her sister's home in another city. The sister was a widow, too, and this seemed to work well for both of them.

The older the woman was when her husband died, the more likely she was to have a chronic, debilitating illness such as diabetes, a heart condition, arthritis, or Parkinson's disease. One widow with Parkinson's disease was completely disabled and in a wheelchair, and she had a homemaker to care for her. She was hospitalized for a period, and the aide continued to visit her in the hospital. This woman had a good attitude toward herself and her situation:

> At first I felt as if the whole world came down on my shoulders, but time dulls the pain and you get used to it. By now I'm used to being a widow.

One woman was considered senile by her family and her doctor. The aide believed that she was only temporarily confused, a result of her husband's sudden death. The aide proved correct in this case. With time and reassurance, the woman's confusion lifted, and she was eager to get involved in a hot-lunch program and to have a visitor come to her house once a week.

Many widows' physical needs were exacerbated by their aloneness. When their husbands were alive, they could help one another and were able to be quite independent. These widows needed a range of helpful interventions. They wanted help from the aide to find adequate housing where they could go out without being fearful of being mugged or robbed. They wanted help getting to medical appointments and getting involved in some activity outside the home. One woman who lived with her daughter was becoming more and more depressed and was not eating. She was alone in the house during the day when her grandchildren were at school and the adults were at work. The aide suggested she come back to her old neighborhood to participate in a hot-lunch program once a week and to play cards with some of her old friends. Her mood changed as she rediscovered her peers.

These women accepted the aide's offer because they needed to share their feelings, to make new friends, and to find ways to stay in charge of their own lives to the extent that this was possible. They did not seem as overwhelmed as younger widows, since they were rarely the first widow in their social network. They understood their crying and their numbness. As one woman said, "I'll be all right. I have to get used to living without him." They wanted not to feel alone and to know that their feelings and needs were typical for women in their situation. In this they identified with the aide:

When I get the cobwebs out of my head, I would like to go back to
work. What can I say, Adele? You know—you're a widow, too.

Widows with Major Psychological Problems
or Drinking Problems

A small group of widows who accepted the offer of help had
serious psychological problems. These were not women who
simply had difficulty managing their lives or even women who
could never rise above their roles as victims of circumstance.
These widows had such severe problems that they came, sometimes involuntarily, to the attention of the police, mental hospi-
tals, and other community agencies. All of them typically maintained a precarious level of adjustment.

The aide quickly identified four women who had problems
with alcoholism. Their drinking was apparent from their behavior. They were eager to engage the aide in solving their problems. Other women had problems that were more difficult to
identify. This group included five women, two of whom the
aide eventually learned had been diagnosed as schizophrenic
and two who had been diagnosed as depressed. A fifth woman
is added here for whom we had no diagnostic label.

The Widow-to-Widow program was designed to prevent
emotional breakdown in a widowed population, and widowhood was seen as a possible precipitant of serious psychological
difficulty. The program was not designed to intervene in long-
standing emotional problems. Not surprisingly, therefore, the
interventions of the widow aide did not seem to make a difference in the psychological outcome for women with prior histories of major psychological difficulty.

Alcohol Problems

One reaction to the death of a spouse may be to begin drinking,
since alcohol is a sedative that a person may use to avoid
confronting reality. When people already have a drinking prob-

lem and lose a spouse, the drinking problem may be exacerbated.

Aides immediately recognized drinking problems in four
women who accepted the offer of help. These women were
accustomed to drinking with their husbands and were already
enmeshed in helping networks of relatives, friends, and agencies
who were concerned about their drinking. Although the aides
rarely asked for the names of grown children or other family
members, in these cases they did, so they could learn more
about what was being done. Once it became apparent that
others were helping and that the widow would not stop drinking, the aide withdrew her offer of help. These accounted for
most of the few instances in which the program withdrew its
offer.

One of these women asked the aide to call a social worker
with whom she was involved, and the aide learned about the
woman's history and about the other people trying to help her.
When the aide called the woman back, the woman was drunk
but denied that she had been drinking. The aide referred her
back to the social worker and did not call her again.

In the three other instances, the aide became involved. She
helped one woman find a better apartment and make her application for welfare. This widow talked about being isolated and
alone now that her husband was dead. The aide suspected that
she had a drinking problem but had no clear evidence. When
things seemed settled, the woman disappeared for a week and
called the aide from the detoxification unit at the city hospital.
The aide then learned about the people who like herself had
been helping this woman and her husband. They too had been
repeatedly disappointed and had withdrawn. Eventually the
aide made a similar decision, since the widow would not stop
drinking.

Another woman was involved in AA, and the aide supported her in this. Within a year, though, the woman was drinking again. In another case, the woman's alcoholism was more
hidden. All the attention was focused on an upstairs neighbor
who was a friend of her husband's. He was clearly a heavy
drinker, and the aide suspected that they drank together. Both

the widow and he had serious physical problems, and his survival required that he stop drinking. They were appealing people, and the aide stayed casually involved with them until the program ended, not really expecting that she was helping beyond showing a neighborly interest. From time to time, they would stop drinking successfully and their health would begin to improve, but they never stopped long enough to do any lasting good.

Major Mental Illnesses

In only one case did we know at the outset of a person's prior history of psychological difficulties. This widow had been hospitalized for treatment of depression, and after her husband died her family had initiated contact with her psychiatrist, fearing she would become ill again. The psychiatrist did not believe she needed any treatment. She was doing well despite her grief and the new demands on her. The widow herself told the aide about her history and her children's current concern, and she and the aide maintained a friendly contact. She was worried that she would get sick again and saw mental illness as a disease that could invade the body without apparent cause and without much control by the individual.

The other psychologically disturbed widows did not share their histories with the aide, and only gradually did the aide become aware of something being wrong. The aide's interventions had little influence, as these women developed symptoms and in two cases were hospitalized. These women were from the beginning more flighty, but only in hindsight did it become clear that their behavior was a reflection of emotional instability. They were more neglectful of their children than might be expected, even from a new widow. These widows were also somewhat unreliable in describing their circumstances, their marriages, and their relations with the outside world.

Initially the aide tried to regard their behavior as normal. She made allowances because of the numbers of children they had, because of inadequate housing, and because of the ways their husbands had died. One died in an automobile accident, two had very painful deaths from cancer, and the fourth was murdered as an innocent bystander to a robbery. Gradually the aide saw that something else was going on.

One woman described herself as a Jackie Kennedy who walked behind her husband's coffin surrounded by her children and not showing her grief. She had eight children. The aide pointed out that it is all right to show one's feelings, and that she in fact did express her feelings. The aide began to realize the tenuous connection between what this widow said and what she did. She could never follow any directions. The aide tried to help this woman organize her day to get the children to school. On some days, if no other adult was in the house, the younger children did not get to school. Over time we recognized that this widow's behavior could not be rationalized, and the aide complained of the impossibility of getting her to follow through:

> I offered to go with her and she never seemed able to set a time. She complained about not having friends but she wouldn't agree to meet anyone. I could understand her just wanting to complain for now. I just kept in touch, and she really looked forward to talking with me. She wept every time we talked almost more than anyone else I've met, and nothing seemed to change over time.

Like others, this widow complained of insomnia and was taking sleeping pills prescribed by the doctor. Like others, she had been very involved with her husband, who had worked nights, so she had very few friends. The difference was that she did not follow through on any suggestions for improvements in her life, and she did not even seem to feel better after talking to the aide. Her husband, as she described him, had cared for the children and done the shopping and was the stabilizing force in the family.

The aide also became aware of the other professionals who were visiting this widow and got her permission to call them. She learned from her calls that the woman was a patient at a local psychiatric home-treatment service, that she was one of several siblings with known mental illness, and that the professional people had been visiting since before she had become a widow. During the year after her husband died, she had be-

come more and more disorganized, and she had been hospitalized after the police found her wandering the streets late one
night. An agency was sending in a woman to clean the house
occasionally, but they could not do this regularly.

Finally, the aide withdrew from the family. She found the
children so hungry for her attention and affection that she
would be upset for days afterward. Short of moving in and
becoming top sergeant for the family, there was nothing she
could do. Although the aide was aware of severe limitations in
the professional help and its failure to address this widow's
problems fully, she knew that she had nothing to add.

In another case where we had no idea of a psychiatric
history, the aide found the widow in very inadequate housing.
Her husband had been murdered just after returning from Vietnam. Another widow the aide was visiting had an apartment for
rent, and the aide introduced the two widows. Not long after
the new widow moved in, she began to frequent bars and bring
men home. She neglected her children and was abusing the
apartment, and her widowed landlady asked her to move. She
then told the landlady about her prior depression and suicide
attempt and hospitalization, but she refused to see that she
might need help in her current situation.

Another woman with grown children and a history of depression had felt totally dependent on her husband:

> We spent all our waking hours together. He worked nights. The
> kids were grown. He never denied me anything. There didn't seem
> to be a need for others. He even went shopping with me.

This woman developed a profound depression about the time
her daughter announced her engagement. She was hospitalized
at a small private psychiatric hospital where she received electroconvulsive therapy, the same treatment she had received
when her husband was alive. She could not recall what had
happened except that she went to pieces:

> I was in the hospital for a month. I continue to see a psychiatrist.
> He does not say much. He does say I am fine. I am on medication
> and I do feel better. I was really able to enjoy my daughter's
> wedding.

In contrast to the other women, this woman used the aide's help to good advantage. She came to an outing and reached out to the other widows there. She enjoyed the aide's call and her friendship. She decided to move and appreciated the aide's encouragement. While she remained indecisive and occasionally difficult to talk with, her behavior showed a clear pattern of appropriate change. She was beginning to live in the present, plan for the future, and act in reference to her changed circumstances. Still, she was like the other women in that none of us could prevent her from becoming mentally ill.

Finally, one widow's deceased husband had had a psychiatric disability and received a pension from the Veterans Administration. With his pension, he could stay home and care for his young children while his wife would take off for weeks at a time. His widow still did this but left the children with babysitters. One child saw a psychiatrist at a local mental health center, but the widow refused to acknowledge that she herself had any problems. The husband had provided the stabilizing force in the family, and the children essentially lost both parents when he died. The widow herself, as if she were another child in the family, had lost her primary caregiver.

In conclusion, in an outreach program it is neither possible nor desirable to screen families in advance to determine their suitability for the program. As a result, the aides met a wide variety of women in equally varied family situations, with different strengths, weaknesses, and abilities to cope. The aides' flexibility and empathy enabled them to engage most of these widows in a relationship that seemed to meet the widows' needs, as will be described in subsequent chapters. However, the aides also found that there were some widows whom they could not help and who would not change. The aides had to learn to pull back from these relationships that were making inappropriate demands on their time, energy, and abilities.

9 Widows Who Refused Help

One-third of the population of widows refused help but agreed to follow-up interviews. These women can be classified into four groups, based on their accommodation at the time of the follow-up interviews. One group, the successful managers, includes five women who had assessed accurately their need for help and still were doing well. A second group of five, the almost-successful managers, thought they might have accepted help if they had been approached differently or later on. A third group, the late accepters, consists of eight women who became involved on their own initiative two or three years after the initial offer of help. A fourth group, the depressed refusers, had by the time of the follow-up developed serious difficulties that seemed minimally traceable to their widowhood. I will discuss each of these groups in turn.

The Successful Managers

For the most part the widows in this group were working. Most had worked before their husbands' deaths because they wanted to supplement the family income or wanted to stay busy after the children grew up, or because the husband was ill and theirs was the primary income. I characterize them as "managers" because they were more or less efficient in their various roles, allowing for different degrees of dependency on others. Only one of these women had small children at home, and after her husband died she worked part time, during the hours when the children were in school. All of these widows were involved in extended family or friendship networks, some of which included widowed friends. They saw their families and friends as helpful and supportive, and they believed that this had made a big difference in the way they had accommodated to their loss. A woman of 50 whose husband had suffered with cancer appreciated her married children's visits, her single son at home, and her upstairs neighbor:

> Everyone has been very good to me. The girl upstairs takes me out. Six years ago she helped me get a job in the phone company.

Working helped many women to accommodate to their loneliness. Initially, many of these women were driven by a need to keep busy, but it also served them well in their eventual accommodation:

> I learned to drive, and work is marvelous. It gives me money to live on and keeps me occupied. I can't sit around and feel sorry for myself.

Coping with Feelings

Most of these women were not accustomed to talking about their feelings, and they did not see that it would necessarily help them now. Many talked more about their grief in their conversations with the follow-up interviewer than they ever had before. Some said they had never let anyone see them cry, and they were proud of this.

One woman, whose husband had died of cancer and who had worked with him in a family business, felt she had lost her confidant as well as a companion:

> I never talked about my problems before, and I won't now. I only talked about my feelings to my husband. I never even talked to my mother.

This widow was not willing to find a replacement for her husband in his confidant role. Few other women in this group spoke of such intimacy with their husbands. This woman still saw herself as her husband's wife, and she talked about how difficult it was to accept herself as a widow. At the same time, her behavior was appropriate to her widowhood. She had moved to a safer neighborhood, had learned to drive, and had new friends with whom she went on holiday trips. Her self-image was involved in the past, but her behavior was present and future oriented. Since behaving differently and appropriately is a first step toward achieving change, the critical issue in deciding what is a good or a bad outcome may be in the way a widow behaves.

All of these women seemed to cope emotionally by holding back and finding ways to avoid their feelings. Sharing feelings in order to understand how they affect behavior was not part of their general style of relationship. With widowhood they confronted overwhelming feelings, feelings that they acknowledged but did not dwell on. In characteristic fashion, they went on to do what needed doing.

Some of the husbands had been sick for long periods of time, up to six years, and others had died suddenly or after a very brief period of illness. Women who had cared for a husband during his illness all talked about their exhaustion at the time of the funeral and sometimes about the sense of relief that his suffering was over. Those whose husbands died suddenly talked about their shock and disbelief. All talked about the initial sense of numbness that they experienced. As one woman described it, an "unreal calmness" seemed to take over.

A 45-year-old woman who worked as a medical technician was married to a heavy drinker who died of cancer and cirrhosis of the liver. She was one of the few people who talked about feeling guilt or blame for her husband's death:

> I think you do [feel guilty] as long as there had been some conflict such as about drinking. It's hard for people to understand, but I still loved him and never wanted to leave him.

This woman talked about her sleepless nights and nervousness after the death. She did not believe in tranquilizers: "A cup of coffee, some aspirins, and a good cry helped. Maybe part of that was feeling sorry for myself." Beyond this, her solution was to keep busy and to not think about it. She had always worked and made most of the family decisions. During the first year after her husband died, she continued her involvement in a church program in which they had both been active and also was kept busy with her family.

Most of these widows preferred not to take tranquilizers. While they all avoided talking about their feelings, they also believed in being aware and did not see how medications would help them in the long run. When they were experiencing the unreality of the impact period, they did not want anything that would compound their difficulty in focusing on reality. As one widow explained:

> I don't believe in them. I was a little nervous. I don't know how you would describe the feeling, but nothing seemed to matter. I lost about 15 pounds at the time. It was unbelievable. He was such a vital man, somebody you thought nothing could ever happen to. But there's life and there's death, and you go on when you have to. The children spent the first six months finding ways to keep me busy, and work was very good from that point of view.

Being involved with family, keeping going, and not allowing too much self-pity seemed to be their style, and it allowed them to change as they needed to.

Accepting and Rejecting Others' Help

Whether the family was small or large, all of these widows remembered people being in and out of the house and recalled how helpful these people were. Often relatives lived in the same building. Some women did not let the family take over and plan the funeral for them; they made all the arrangements:

> I was exhausted from running to the hospital; death was almost a relief. My children were very helpful, but I arranged the funeral myself.

Some women simply felt they could not count on others:

> When I was young the whole neighborhood would rally, but not any more. Everyone seemed too busy trying to make a living and getting things. We forget others.

Even when others were willing to help, as was the usual pattern, these women were more comfortable doing things for themselves.

Most women shared with their older children the responsibility for arranging the funeral and for informing relatives. Part of the managerial talent of some women was to know when to let others take over:

> My son informed all the relatives. The funeral director was a friend of the family. He came and took charge of everything. My husband was very active in the church, and one of the priests came who knew him very well. He visited quite often afterward.

This woman and her husband had been inseparable and had done everything as a couple. She found herself more nervous, with a loss of appetite and some sleeplessness, but what was most difficult was

> . . . just getting used to his not being around. Working nights, as I have done for many years, now keeps me occupied. I was in a state of shock. I still had teenaged children at home. Having to provide for them and having the emotional support of my family helped me adjust.

Such a self-reliant, optimistic woman would not likely fail to cope with her normal daily routines. Indeed, her solution was to be involved and busy. Unlike those who accepted help, this woman's family, church, and friends were available and remained helpful over time. Although this woman was doing well like others in the group, she knew her life would never be the same:

> You don't forget. You get used to it. Sometimes I still think of him as here.

One of her major concerns for the future was to maintain good health, since she had to keep the house and family together. This was a concern for many women as they thought about their futures alone.

Many of these women had always been the caretakers in their family, and this influenced how they coped as well as how they received an offer of help. They were accustomed to taking care of others, unaccustomed to being taken care of, and had always solved their own problems; this did not change with their husbands' deaths. For one or two whose husbands had had long illnesses, an extra caretaking role was thrust on them, but they were willing to accept it:

> I had to assume all the burdens when we found out that he had a brain tumor that couldn't be operated on.

A woman who worked as an administrative secretary found that extra responsibility helped after the death:

> I was always the one everyone came to with their troubles. Right after my husband died my son married and brought his bride home to live so they could finish college. She got pregnant and now I am a grandmother. It keeps me very busy, but I guess I like it that way.

This was not a woman to accept the help of others:

> I always solved my own problems and I wasn't going to change now.

For some women, being helped might mean losing independence. Even a 38-year-old mother of three preferred to go on without help:

> It might confuse you more . . . I like to think by myself and make my own decisions.

Like others, this woman may have assumed that receiving help meant getting advice that she would have to follow. She had no concept of a helping relationship as a give-and-take in which

a person could accept or reject information and guidance.
Women with this view of help did not accept the offer of help
from the Widow-to-Widow program.

All of these women believed that no one else could really
solve their problems and that they themselves had to work out
their problems. Most could see the value of talking with another
widow, and they speculated that this might give a woman a
push to get out of the house or a way to make new friends.
Although they saw that this service would be important for a
woman alone, they themselves did not have the need for it.
Often these women knew other widows who were as helpful to
them as the aide might have been:

> I don't really talk to anyone about how I feel. My son takes care of
> any minor problems that arise. I have a group of widowed friends. I
> do many things with them. Sometimes you get teary and feel a
> great loneliness. You get over it but you never forget; I guess in
> part it is getting accustomed to it. Widow-to-Widow is a great idea
> for people with no family or friends to support them. But I didn't
> need that.

Since these women all worked, they had no need for vocational counseling. They felt that work was very helpful and that
many women would need some assistance in finding work or
some retraining for entering the labor market.

In many ways, the successful managers are models of successful coping over time. They demonstrate a range of adequate
accommodations, in contrast to the accommodations of the
other three groups.

The Almost-Successful Managers

Another group of women who refused help reported during the
follow-up interview that they could have used help later on,
although they never did call the aide or respond to the program's periodic invitations to group activities.

These women differed from the successful managers in the
way they responded to their grief, in their ability to meet their

own needs in the long run, and in their understanding of the offer of help. The almost-successful managers were all in their middle to late fifties, except for one in her late forties. Their children were grown, and more of them lived alone than did the successful managers. They had a similar independent style, but it seemed less effective for them, perhaps because they were less able to initiate and sustain relationships.

Like the successful managers, these women talked of their children helping with the funeral and afterwards, of their numbness and shock, of how their work helped a good deal, and so forth. As they continued to talk, though, they made revealing comments such as, "I was always a loner" and "I never bother with the neighbors; they give you a lot of trouble." Their style of relating had a quality of distance, and they were more suspicious and less open to opportunities and friendships.

These women reconsidered their refusal of help when three years later they were still mourning. Although they had moved beyond impact and were no longer numb, they seemed stuck in the recoil period, acutely aware of their pain. One woman said,

> Work helps a great deal. I'd go nuts otherwise. But over time, my feelings have not changed. I get blue and lonesome and feel as if I'm dead inside. My feelings stay right here and I feel as if they can't come out. I was thinking of learning to drive but I haven't yet.

This woman went out with single female friends but did not think she would fit easily in a mixed group.

Many women felt dissatisfied with how they had managed their grief:

> It's two years later, and I think about him a lot. I always see people who resemble him. Administrative decisions are the hardest. I still have trouble making those. Thank God we moved just before he died so I don't have to see him in everything in the house. Every once in a while when I face a problem I can't manage, I look at the walls and cry, "Where are you?"

These women seemed not to have given up their roles as wives or to have found new ways of solving problems by themselves. While successful managers seemed to do this by themselves, as an "act of will," these women thought that talking would have some value:

> I generally don't talk about my problems, and that's no good.

> I think that talking can help. I talk to my girlfriend, but she always takes the initiative. I wouldn't call her.

> Maybe if I had talked it through I would be having an easier time now.

> I have my sister with whom I share everything. Otherwise, I don't know what I would have done. Everybody needs someone.

These women were less repressed than the successful managers and closer to their real feelings. They did not have the will or the aptitude to be so busy that they could avoid their feelings by being active. Although one would assume that these women might have been receptive to help from a widow aide, they refused. Their refusals did not seem to reflect their perceived lack of need, but their general suspiciousness of others and their reluctance to admit they had a need. Such an admission would have upset their image of independence and self-reliance. The woman who talked to her friend only when the friend called saw herself as very shy. Others saw visits from friends or neighbors as burdens, requiring them to act the hostess and take care of the guest. As one said:

> I felt I did not have time to make refreshments and entertain them. I work and I am really tired when I come home. I was confused, and I was trying to get things straightened out. I wanted to be independent.

This woman could not get involved in spontaneous interactions that might have helped her sort out her feelings, because she believed this would have added to her problems. Another woman, who had always pursued her own interests, when she was widowed felt that she wanted to be involved only if she could help. At the time she had no energy for this. To admit need and receive help would have seemed to rob her of her sense of independence.

This group's reluctance to accept help may have reflected their natural mode of reacting to social initiatives. One woman explained her response to the aide's call this way:

> I felt intruded upon. I got the idea this is a clubby thing done by rich ladies. That's not for me. Maybe if she'd come back in a couple of months, or if she had been a little less eager to help, I might have responded. I'm really a very private person.

And yet, aside from a sister, she had no peer confidantes. Her great loneliness came out when she extended the follow-up interview for four hours, and this after she had to be talked into the interview in the first place. She explained:

> The whole idea seemed so strange, and I was so surprised when the aide first called. I've read about it in the paper since then. I wish she had called me back. I thought of calling, but I didn't want to bother her. I think now I like the idea of having another widow to talk with. My husband was an alcoholic. Life is much better without him. I can plan ahead and make progress without his undoing it. However, the kids are growing. When I'm left alone, I really miss my husband. I have no single friends.

Once she read about the program in the newspaper, it had more legitimacy for her. She then saw it as something that might have helped her cope better, but, like the others, she made no move to call or to respond to any of the invitations she received.

Another woman thought she might have had an easier time if she had talked things over with the aide who contacted her:

> My daughter wants me to get involved after I retire next year. I have a friend who joined a widows' group. It's wonderful—they do so many things.

The help that this woman and the others needed and wanted at follow-up was to extend their social network. (The interviewer told these women about all the groups for the widowed in this area so that they could join if they wished.)

On the whole, the women in this group were doing well, although they seemed to lack the drive, will, and optimism that characterized the successful managers. They showed less acceptance of the sense of loss, and this feeling still seemed to encompass their lives. Relatives were less responsive or viewed as less helpful. The Widow-to-Widow program had offered them many opportunities to get involved, and we cannot be sure that more aggressive efforts would have engaged them.

The Late Accepters

A very small group of only eight women did get involved after initially refusing. These women also had the quality of wanting to be independent, of not taking tranquilizers, and of being involved with immediate and extended family. All but one of them worked. Only one handled her feelings easily, was aware of them and accepted them; the others to varying degrees avoided talking about feelings. All at first felt that they had no need for help and refused the aide's offer. Two women were abrupt in their refusal. One said, "I'm able to be on the move. I don't sit around all day." The other stated that she had family and a daughter and was annoyed that anyone thought she would need someone else. Two years later she found herself rejected and confused by her family. She was angry that they wanted her to see a psychiatrist. Then after she read in the newspaper about a meeting sponsored by the Widow-to-Widow program, she came to the group meeting and found them very helpful.

Only one called the aide directly when her needs changed. She had broken her hip and seemed to have alienated her married children. She wanted the aide to come talk with her, shop for her, and do things for her so she would not have to pay to have them done. These expectations were unrealistic, and ultimately she felt let down by the aide, who never could provide her with all the services she requested.

The other women found their way back to the program when they joined a club for the widowed. The aides who initially had called them also went to this club. One of these women then became a volunteer at the Widowed Service Line.

She had come to the club at her brother's encouragement (he lived with her) so that she could meet other people with similar interests. She felt she had managed her own grief fairly well, and when the chance came volunteered to help others.

Another woman had just remarried and had refused initially because she was too exhausted and talking was not her way of dealing with things:

> I was very tired after my husband's long illness. I had so many problems, things to cope with. I had to take care of my father-in-law. I just felt that I couldn't get involved with a group of widows. I didn't understand how the service worked. Dorothy tried to make it clear that she just called to talk, and I could call her back, but I never did. When I met her at Arch Street, I really talked and talked. I even called her up to tell her how I was coming out of this hard time I was having. I really never liked to talk or think about things.
>
> I just felt useless. I had no one to take care of. Suddenly you discover you are not needed. Even Dorothy couldn't understand, because she had children to worry about. In that case you think of them, of their sorrow. Even when grown children try to help it's not the same. They have their own lives and problems. My brother-in-law took care of the funeral. It's better if you have someone do that for you.
>
> I love to dance. Going out to dances helped me a lot. It also helped to meet other widowed people. It's not that you talk a lot about your problems, but there is common understanding and empathy.

This woman's need to talk two and a half years later may have been due in part to the pain having gone away and in part to her wanting to review the past as she moved into a new relationship. Her new husband was different from her first husband in that he wanted to involve her in decisions and the like. She may have learned new ways of coping in such a qualitatively different relationship.

The main difference between the group that felt a need but did not act (almost-successful managers) and the group that acted (late accepters) was one of degree. The group that eventually acted found themselves in sufficient pain or need that they had to find new resources and new involvements. They also had the will to act. The ones who did not act neither felt as much discomfort nor were sufficiently energetic socially to seek out a club or help from a stranger. They were more suspicious and more reticent.

The Depressed Refusers

Four women who refused the offer of help at the time felt they were doing well but thought the program was a good idea. Since they had children at home or nearby and they did not have any problems, they felt they did not need such a service:

> At the time I was doing good. I didn't feel that I needed anyone. I was keeping busy and I didn't feel up to meeting anyone new.

All of them said they would call if the need arose. These women may have been reticent to involve themselves in new friendships since they were not particularly outgoing or involved in any activities outside their families. Only one of them was working (as a legal secretary), and she had done this for several years before her husband died. These women did not think of calling the aide and did not respond to any of the invitations they received.

At the time of the follow-up interviews, these women were all in varying stages of depression. Although they were still carrying on with normal routines, they did not have a sense of well-being or much hope for the future. One woman had to be coaxed into the follow-up interview, agreeing only if the researcher would meet her at her office. Another woman's son-in-law, who was a probation officer, talked her into seeing the interviewer. Help was generally thrust on them by their concerned family; these women did not seem to be coping alone, and they used tranquilizers and found them helpful in some way.

There was a typical pattern that began to emerge for these women, after their husbands' deaths:

> They [children] kept giving me phenobarbital, but I felt I didn't need them. I was like in a dream. It hit me later.

> I was numb, in a state of shock. He had had a heart condition, but I did not expect his death; I was out of it. My relatives took care of the funeral and calling people.

Such behavior and responses were not characteristic of the way these women had responded prior to the death:

> I went to work when my husband had his first heart attack, so I could support myself if I had to.

> I made all the decisions. I got the bills and his pay. We used to talk over things about the children. He was an easygoing man, not the drinking type.

These women had been competent, planful people who for the most part had managed their own lives, but they did not seem to be doing this at the time of the follow-up. One woman attributed her change to the quality of the relationship she had had with her husband:

> It would have been better if we hadn't been so close. We did everything together.

Much of these women's energy had been taken up in being their husbands' wives. Even when they worked, it was because of the husband's illness and his possible inability to continue to support his family. Over the three years since their husbands' deaths, their children were growing up or had grown up and no longer needed them.

Three factors emerge as critical to understanding these women's depressions and their marginal accommodations to grief. First is the ambivalent quality in their relationships with grown or growing children; second is the importance of the wife and mother role to their sense of well-being; and third is a possible reawakening of old wounds around unresolved dependency problems. Several case examples illustrate these factors and the ways they can intertwine to create serious difficulties.

As for relationships with the children, the most extreme case makes a good example. She was a 52-year-old woman who lived in a housing project with a very high crime rate. When her husband first died, her children were still living at home and she got a job as a clerk in a nearby shopping center. Later on, when her children married and she was alone, she began dating a man she met at work. At her children's insistence she stopped seeing him; she traces her depression to that time:

> If I had slept with him it would have been harder to give him up. I started to get very nervous. I became scared to go out. They were talking of closing the store because of vandalism. I was on tranquilizers, so I stopped working and went on welfare.
>
> My daughter insisted I go see the psychologist at the health center. She [the psychologist] gave me Librium and Valium. She recognized, too, that the world is frightening, especially around here. It was the wrong time to be alone. She couldn't really help me solve some of these problems. I had accepted my husband's death; after all, he had been sick for so long. I considered it a gift that I had him that long. I need to move now, but where can I go with my income?
>
> My biggest worry is that I am alone and no one wants me or needs me. I'm ready to go back to work, but it is too dangerous to go out.

As this woman was building a new life, her children, for reasons that are unclear, interfered. Having followed their advice, she found herself in an untenable situation. She had created a new dependency on them when she followed their advice, but the role reversal did not work because they did not care for her successfully. This, combined with the real dangers in her community, made her helpless and therefore depressed.

A related pattern entails the children's willingness to support their mother and to allow her to transfer her dependency from her husband to them. Two women in very different life situations exemplify this pattern. Both seem to have depended on their husbands for everything and then to have transferred that dependency to their grown children. In both instances, the children were willing to accept their mother's dependency. Both women still were mourning at the time of follow-up. They had remained their husbands' wives and made no life changes toward accommodating to their losses.

One woman, aged 57, was living in very poor conditions on Social Security and some income from her unmarried daughter, who lived with her. Her household seemed depressed, and the interviewer wondered if the widow might be drinking. She still cried herself to sleep at night, talking to her husband's pictures. She said she did not want to talk with another widow because "all they do is talk about the dead." Yet this was what she herself did much of the time. The two married daughters who lived in the same building seemed willing to support their mother in her depressed lifestyle. Her single daughter was willing to live with her in what can only be termed squalid conditions. The program could do little to change this complex set of relationships and conditions.

Another woman who showed this pattern was a 45-year-old widow who spoke very poor English. She had migrated from Poland some years earlier, and her entire social life revolved around the Polish-American Club and the church. She had lost her son two years before her husband died, and she and her husband had worked together in a factory. While she tried to continue to work after his death, she found herself too nervous and upset. She had always taken medicine for her nerves, and she felt better once she was not working. Her grief was compounded by her son's death, and in many ways she felt that she had already "cried herself out" over that. Her other children were true supports and friends to her, as was her large extended family. Her greatest hope was to see the children through college. In the tradition of her culture, she probably will remain her husband's wife and widow all her life. While this widow received much from her children, she also seemed to give a good deal. In her case, the interdependency worked well. It allowed for the growth and development of the young people and sustained the widow, albeit in a somewhat depressed state.

Other women had invested their lives in the roles of mother and wife and, finding themselves no longer needed, felt helpless:

We did everything together. I miss him very much. What could anyone do? No one can help. Weekends are worse. The children are busy with their own lives. I never went out alone and I don't now.

I don't enjoy cooking or keeping house any more. There's no one who cares about it. I don't even like to crochet now. There is no one to give me encouragement.

These women neither developed new interests nor found satisfactory dependencies or interdependencies with their children, family, or friends. Typically these women had always coped by being in charge and running the show within the family context. They felt independent and self-sufficient in this way and had never needed to find interests or involvements outside the family context.

Once widowed, these women tried to make new, independent lives, and either their children would resist or they themselves might become ill. One widow who became ill had started to work just before her husband got sick and had worked daily for a year after he died. After she got ill, she could not work and therefore faced serious financial problems. In addition, her son was causing her some worry:

He is going out on his own. He has long hair. I think he smokes marijuana. Years ago a mother had jurisdiction even if the child was 41. That's not true now, and I really worry about him.

These widows were not in charge of their lives any more, and they could not count on their children either. In this regard, they may have had more reason to fear dependency than the women whose children appeared more reliable.

One widow, who seemed to have a comfortable relationship with her children (the interviewer described her as warm and motherly), worried a good deal about becoming a burden on them:

I'm used to being on my own. My mother died when I was 15. There was the Depression during the early years of our marriage, and so I am used to having to provide for myself.

She received Social Security and worked part time in the marking room of a department store so she would have money to buy little things for her grandchildren. She attributed much of her current depression to the close relationship she had had with her husband, and she seemed unable, despite her own determination, to fight off her sadness:

> It is hard to say that I am finished mourning. It is a big empty house full of memories. The nights are hardest. I'm fighting to cut down on the tranquilizers . . .

This widow's lack of success may have been due to unresolved grief over her mother's death. In so many other ways, she was like the successful managers. Her adjustment to her mother's death was the only way she differed, and this may have accounted for her poor accommodation. Like the other women, she did not see talking as a way of solving problems, but she did have widow friends with whom she commiserated over feelings of loneliness.

The deterioration for these women seemed to have occurred over the years after their husbands died: as the children grew up and moved, as they became aware of their own increasing age and disabilities, and as they confronted the fact that they might become dependent. They were correct in their initial assessment that they did not need the aide's help. They were not predisposed to call for help later on, and any contact the aide may have had with them subsequently was during the period when they were coping with the normal upset of the first year of bereavement. Perhaps we had indications of these widows' future need in their use of tranquilizers, in their inability to participate in the funeral arrangements, and in their early experience of parental loss.

Conclusions

Based on this limited review, most people who refused help were correct in their appraisal of their need at the time we offered help. Furthermore, most were able to manage their grief, and we might conclude that the most needy were not in the refusal group. What becomes apparent, however, is the importance of timing in the offer of help. For some widows, two or three years later may be the best time to offer assistance, new opportunities for friendship, and a chance to expand the social network. As children grow up, as the widow herself gets older, or as she develops a disability, her aloneness becomes an acute problem for her. If she is not already part of a larger group of successful managers, she needs someone to teach her how to cope and to help her learn what she cannot learn by herself.

IV Helping

10 Ways of Helping

The aides offered help in the form of information, friendship, and concrete assistance. Their style was personal, and they made themselves available in the manner of an informed and concerned neighbor or close friend. The long-term goal of the aide's help was to enable the widow to change her sense of identity, to move initially from the role of wife to the role of widow, and then to move from the role of widow to new roles. In the words of one aide, "Eventually you begin to think of yourself as a formerly married woman."

Help had to be available in a way that was responsive to the widow's immediate needs, and the way of helping had to change as the widow's needs changed. The aides did not meet widows on a regular schedule or structure their interactions in any formal way. The aide and the widow met in person in the widow's home, they talked at length on the phone, they went out to a movie or on an outing, and on occasion the widow came to the aide's home for a visit. They shared coffee, they shared tears, and in several instances they became close friends. Sometimes people met once a week. Most often they kept in touch by phone several times a month after the initial contact. Sometimes they would not meet in person for months at a time.

The first things the new widow asked of the aide was how her husband had died and how she had managed. Although the psychological literature on helping the bereaved emphasizes the need to talk about the circumstances of the death, the aides found that widows were most interested in knowing how someone else had survived and in learning how she had managed. Over time, the aides encountered three themes in widows' needs for help: independence, loneliness, and social life. Many women had to learn to make decisions independently. In the words of a 45-year-old mother of three teenagers, "The biggest decision I had ever made was what loaf of bread to buy." Widows also needed to learn to be alone. Almost every woman who accepted help was concerned with the silence in her home. Finally, widows needed help in making new friends and getting along socially:

> I don't get invited out by our couple friends anymore. I'm not always comfortable with them. It makes me feel even lonelier.

The Telephone

The telephone was an important tool for helping. With it, the aide could be available in the evening to women who worked; for some working women, the telephone was the primary contact. In addition, the aides were not always comfortable visiting in some neighborhoods at night. The telephone also enabled the aide to be in touch during a crisis or at a particularly low moment. In one widow's words:

> I couldn't sleep; I needed to talk so I called. We talked until one in the morning. That got me through a really tough time.

Each aide had a separate telephone in her home, paid for by the program, so that she could be available without tying up her own telephone and cutting off family and friends.

Some widows used the telephone contact for complaining. They didn't really seem to want to help themselves. Some women called often but would never agree to a visit. One woman finally said that her house was not fit to visit. She had arthritis and was more comfortable not having to pick up in order to "entertain." Others who used only the telephone said they were too busy to visit or go out:

> Please don't come now. My daughter is getting married and, with work, I am too busy.

Some women were not comfortable with face-to-face encounters but needed to talk as much as others. The telephone gave them some anonymity while allowing them a level of intimacy they could tolerate. One woman whose husband had committed suicide said she was going to take a civil service test and would not be home for a visit. She thought the program was a good idea and was eager for the aide to call back. Although they subsequently spoke often on the phone, the widow put off a face-to-face meeting. She would allude to her husband's sudden death on the telephone but did not elaborate. She would talk about her job hunting, her activities in a bowling league and in church, and her children. She used the aide as a sounding-board as she built a new life for herself and her six children, who ranged in age from 10 to 20. The aide and the widow never met and never talked about the meaning the suicide may have had for the family. Perhaps this was something the widow could not do; so she protected herself by limiting her contact to the telephone, where it may have been easier to limit the range of conversation.

Several other women accepted help only over the telephone. Some of these women seemed sufficiently involved with friends, family, and children and over the long run had no need for any other contact with the program. These women did not necessarily shift gears or change their lifestyle. Rather, friends and family seemed to take the place of their husbands, and they were able to manage in this way. Other women felt so busy with work and family that they had "no time to think." Furthermore, they did not want to meet other widows or have reminders that their husbands were dead. They enjoyed talking, but after awhile they simply had no reason to remain in touch. The difference between these people and those who refused was their willingness to be neighborly within certain limits.

Some widows eventually met the aide much later, after months of talking on the telephone. Usually this happened after a year, when they wanted to extend their social network. Then they would meet the aide at a social event sponsored either by the Widow-to-Widow program or by another group the aide told them about.

For some women the telephone provided the means of keeping in touch for a short time until they had a chance to meet. Still others were not sure when they might get more involved, but they were helped by simply knowing that help would be available when they needed and wanted it:

> One of my children picks me up every evening for supper. They need to be with me now. When they don't need me as much I'd like to get involved.

Home Visits

When the aide visited the home, the women most often talked in the kitchen, with the living room being the next most frequent place. Some women had coffee ready, while others were too disorganized. Many women were not concerned about their homes being "in order," and some were still in their housecoats as if they had just gotten out of bed. One woman was ill when the aide visited, and the aide made her something to eat. The aides became comfortable with sitting down to talk regardless of the physical conditions they encountered.

Even though the program was virtually unknown in the community during its first year, very few women were really suspicious of the aide. Some women had talked on the telephone and already had satisfied themselves that the aide was not a salesperson or a religious missionary. Several women arranged a telephone signal with a friend, as a way to indicate that everything was all right. One woman had her brother-in-law stay around long enough to see that the aide was a trustworthy person who only wanted to help. Most women saw the aide as someone who cared:

> It was nice to know that someone was interested in what was happening to me.

Friends, neighbors, and children were often in and out, so these meetings were rarely very private. Nonetheless, this did not seem to affect the quality of the conversation. Though aides at first worried about what they would say and how long they should stay, these were never problems. How long to stay was dictated by what else the widow had planned for the day. Aides found that their first visits usually lasted at least two hours. What to say was not an issue since the new widow had a great need to talk. Her husband had been dead for about six weeks to two months, and her family and friends were becoming impatient with her concerns. Even more important than this, she was happy to have another widow to talk with:

> A widow needs friendship, someone to talk to. Dorothy was a good listener, and that's what I needed.

Since we kept no process notes on these visits, we cannot reconstruct exactly what took place and what was said. We do know that aides simply took it for granted that widows would cry when talking about their husbands.

The prototype for the visit was that of a neighbor dropping in. The aides saw the help they offered as an extension of what they would do for a neighbor. While they were paid, they did not think of helping in this way as something one would typically do for "work." They did it out of their concern for others and their willingness to give. Nonetheless, they did develop different styles of helping.

At one extreme was a style similar to the professional–client relationship, and at the other a relationship more like friendship (Abrahams, 1976). The professional–client relationship implied some distance between the helper and the one seeking help; the helper felt knowledgeable about the adjustment process and wanted to pass on information to the seeker of help. The friendship relationship implied that the helper and the one seeking help had an equality of feelings and experience. Between these two extremes were a range of styles in which varying needs were met in various ways on both sides of the helping relationship.

To help only as a friend would have been difficult. As one aide said, "How many new friends can I include in my life?" Most of the helping was based on mutuality complemented by an ability to stand outside as "the elder stateswoman" with the longer experience. At the same time, several of the aides, by the end of the program, had developed an extensive friendship and acquaintance network in which they and some dozen widows they had helped were equal participants and partners. The flexibility of the program made it easy for the aide to change her relationship with the widow as the widow's needs changed.

The chapters that follow will describe how the helping process was related to widows' changing needs during various phases of their bereavement. Chapter 11 describes the impact period and how the aide helped the widow begin to confront her loss and the changes in her life. Chapter 12 describes the recoil period and how the aide helped the widow to accept her pain and begin to see options for coping with her changed situation. Chapter 13 focuses on accommodation and how the aide supported the widow in redirecting her life and consolidating her life changes.

Group Activities

Much of the program's help took the form of group activities, which met a variety of needs for the widows. They offered opportunities to meet other widows, to learn more about dealing with particular issues, to network and make exchanges, to begin forming new relationships, and eventually to help others. Meetings and social events also helped deal with the aide's question regarding how many friends she could have in her life; in effect, they extended and enhanced her ability to help.

Aides organized the group meetings and invited all of the widows. These meetings dealt with questions that widows had raised: what to do with their leisure, what was involved in getting back to work, and how to help children understand their father's death. The meetings brought together the widows who had not seen an aide in person as well as those whom the aides had come to know quite well. Invitations to meetings gave the aide an easy excuse for calling the widow and a realistic way of meeting some of her need to find new people and new connections with the community.

Many of the group activities were primarily social. For some, going to the movies or a cookout was just a way of being entertained and getting out:

I won't talk to other widows. They cry too much. I have my own
troubles. I want to go dancing and have a good time.

More often, however, the social occasion not only provided the
opportunity to go out but also gave widows a chance to meet
other widows, people with whom they often developed lasting
friendships.

11 Impact

During the impact stage, the widow feels numb and has a sense of unreality around her. At the same time, she has many concrete tasks to keep her active in the real world, and getting through all these chores gives her time to let what has happened sink into her consciousness. Friends and family may be close by at this time, and usually neither they nor the widow realize that this is only the beginning of a long and painful process.

During this period, the widow needs to allow her numbness to lift and to recognize at some level that a new reality exists. The Widow-to-Widow program hypothesized that someone in her own situation—another widow—might help her deal with these early tasks. If the new widow could allow another widow into her life, thus acknowledging that she might have something in common with a widow, then she could begin to deal with her pain and her changing needs.

It Didn't Really Happen, Did It?

One woman's husband collapsed at the age of 35 at a church picnic and was dead by the time he reached the hospital. His widow naturally was shocked and later was unable to recall many of the surrounding circumstances:

> We went out as a family, and the next thing I knew I was in an ambulance taking my husband to the hospital. He was already

149

dead and I guess I knew it. I didn't see my children again until after the funeral. Someone must have taken them to my mother's. That's where I found them. I really didn't know what hit me. Maybe I still don't.

It is no surprise that this type of death leaves the widow in a state of shock and disbelief. After a long illness, however, the death has been anticipated and sometimes may be an almost welcome relief from the agony of a deathwatch:

His attacks were so bad he would almost choke to death. It's the worst thing that can happen to anyone. You have to live with it to realize it.

Depression, or perhaps more accurately, a letdown, may set in from the exhaustion:

We were worn out from caring for him. We couldn't get any sleep.

Even after a long illness the widow feels numb and unbelieving, though for a shorter time. She has not anticipated how she will feel once his pain is over and the door is finally closed:

He suffered so much. I was glad it was over for him, but I didn't expect to feel this way . . .

She had not expected to feel so much grief, and she is surprised to feel numbness and disbelief:

Even though I knew it was going to happen [that he would die] I still had this feeling. Even at the funeral I couldn't believe I was really dressing the children to get ready to go to my own husband's funeral.

She may be surprised even though she knew that death was imminent. There are different ways of knowing; that is, a widow may know but not know:

I had to read the notice in the paper before it penetrated.

None of these widows had anticipated what it would be like to be bereaved, even though many had time to anticipate how they might manage. Some had talked with their husbands about the impending death, while others had avoided any discussion. The circumstances of the death did not seem to temper the feelings associated with the real loss. The period of numbness and disbelief might be foreshortened in the case of a long illness, but widows still had to deal with grief and with what it means to be a widow (Silverman, 1972).

For all widows, no matter how the husband died, the most difficult thing was to think of themselves as widows. Just as the new widow finds it difficult to believe that her husband is dead although intellectually she may know it very well, she does not yet see a relationship between her new legal status as a widow and her sense of self:

> I could not use the word "widow," I could not believe that it applied to me and that he was really gone.

A young widow with very young children may feel this especially acutely:

> I accepted it. He had been very ill for a year. I couldn't understand why, but I was able to accept that he was gone. What was hardest for me was accepting it for me. Here I was, 23, girls my own age were just finishing college or out working a few years, and I was a widow.

Whether they had been prepared for the death or it came suddenly, the new widows felt the ascription "widow" had no place in their sense of who they were. One woman in her mid-fifties, whose husband had died suddenly the month before, recalled her reaction to the letter from the Widow-to-Widow program:

> I thought, what an awful word to call me. I threw the letter away. I didn't think that the word widow had anything to do with me.

Nevertheless, this woman talked with the aide at length on the telephone. A woman's willingness to talk with the aide may have little to do with her ability to identify herself with the widowed aide at that time, nor may it be related to a conscious sense of what her needs are. The new widow usually feels in some way detached from herself; she is both aware and unaware of herself:

> At the funeral I just sat there. It was like standing outside and watching.

> People told me I was in shock. As I look back I guess they were right, but I didn't know it at the time. I thought that I was fine and in touch with everything. Only later when people talked about the funeral I realized my brother and sister had done everything.

New widows do not suddenly become helpless. Although they may feel they are not "in charge" of themselves at this time, they find themselves beginning with the funeral, making decisions that they never thought they could make:

> If someone had suggested to me that I could negotiate a funeral I would have said never.

One widow said that she "grew up at that moment."

Few of the widows could think clearly enough to know what they needed. Some found that taking care of details in the house, applying for pensions, and so forth helped them keep touch with reality. Some focused on sending thank you notes to people, for their consideration during this period:

> I wrote 200 thank you notes. I had to do it myself. I had trouble finding words and sometimes it took a long time to get even one finished. But it was important to me that I do it by myself. I needed to focus on something that I could do.

Initial Contacts

Some women put the aide off when she called. One woman called the aide to tell her not to come, saying that she was not feeling well and was feeling nervous since her husband had died very suddenly. As they talked, she asked the aide how her husband had died and learned that the aide's husband also had died unexpectedly. The new widow then asked about the aide's children and finally changed her mind about the visit:

> I didn't feel like talking, but now that I have talked with you, I want to see you. Come tomorrow.

Another widow who had told the aide not to come found herself talking at length on the telephone. She laughed when she realized what was happening, since she had been so direct in saying, "I don't want to talk about it." Still, she preferred the telephone at that time:

> I don't mind talking over the phone, but to have someone come in to talk or to meet you on the street is too difficult. I can't face it.

This widow had opened the door to acknowledging her grief and the fact of her husband's death, but she needed time. Nothing would be gained by having her face her situation all at once. The aide could legitimate these feelings and be there in whatever way would be helpful to this woman.

Some who initially refused a visit later regretted it:

> I was in a state of shock. I had no idea what I needed. I thought I was fine. I yelled at Dorothy that I didn't need her. That was a big mistake. I needed her, but I didn't know it.

Women who were not working were usually pleased to see the aide, and some of them easily saw the value of the relationship:

> I had never met this woman, yet she stayed for about an hour to an hour and a half. We just sat down and talked. We had coffee and all. I liked her very much, and I thought she was a good help for me. I was feeling pretty depressed, you know. It's very hard to explain. You feel as though nobody, no matter who, really understands. Still, you take another widow and they know, they can share, they know what the experience is. Not that she would tell me what to do, but just to be able to open up pathways.

While many women who were not working and at home were still caring for young children, others were older. One whose husband had lingered with cancer for many years talked about how important it was to be able to talk with someone who could really understand:

> She [the aide] was very nice. I needed someone who understood what I was feeling, and I guess there is nobody like another widow. She understood how I felt, you know, even though I knew that he was going to die.

Widows were surprised by the depth of their feelings, and knowing that others had had the same experience helped them to accept these feelings as legitimate:

> I never thought there was another widow as young as me until I saw Dorothy. I thought that I was the only one in the world. I guess I needed to know that I wasn't. And she had the energy to come visiting as well. I could not anticipate that I would ever be where she was.

Seeing another widow who obviously was managing well was encouraging:

> Actually, I wasn't listening to anything she [the aide] was saying. I was just looking at her talking. It amazed me that anyone who had ever felt like I do could talk like that. I must have still been in a state of shock. I couldn't talk to anyone about how I felt and here she was. . . . Now that I think about it, it gave me hope.

The aide had to establish not only her own widowhood but also that she was someone beyond a lady bountiful. The aide shared the widow's roots in the community, perhaps her ethnic origins, and sometimes friends in common:

> Once she [the new widow] discovered we were both French Canadians and that I had grown up in this community, she relaxed and we just talked. She put up some tea. It was two hours before I left.

Dealing with Practical Matters

During these initial visits, most of the time was spent talking about practical things such as pension benefits:

> This widow didn't know that she was entitled to VA benefits. I found the address for her and reviewed the procedures. I offered to drive her down but she had a friend who would go. I warned her that they might make her feel like they were doing her a favor, but she was entitled to the money. To make sure she got everything she was entitled to, I explained how I had handled them.

Some women had not yet gotten their Social Security checks and needed to work out a budget or apply for welfare until the money came in. Some were exhausted from caring for their husbands and working to support the family; they needed a rest:

> Now that I have Social Security I'm quitting my job for a while. I need time to rest.

Talking about money sometimes seemed an affirmation of life:

> It made me think about what was needed to go on living (even if I wasn't sure I wanted to), and it reminded me that in spite of it all that's what I have to do.

Other women, especially older women, wanted to talk about going to work. Some needed to know about filling out job applications, and the aide could warn the new widow about how it might feel to check the word "widow" on the application. Work had many meanings for older women, and some faced the double bind of not being able to focus well enough to do a good job but needing to get out of the house and make money to pay the bills:

> I need something to keep me busy, but I can't really concentrate on anything. Still I have to pay my bills.

Those with no experience working had to learn even such simple things as reading employment sections of the newspaper.

Social Security and insurance benefits gave some widows a financial security they had not had before. The aide might show the widow how to budget and make long-term financial plans, now that she had a regular income. One young woman, whose husband was killed in an automobile accident shortly after he got his first job, thought she would have to abandon any hope of leaving the neighborhood and having a home of her own. The aide gave her specific advice and a new sense of hope:

> I told her that with the insurance money she would collect she did have a down payment. I would feel funny doing this if my husband was alive, but under the circumstances I told her to go to her local bank and explain her situation to the manager. He would clarify what loans she could get and if she could afford a house. I did the same thing after my husband died. The widow did it and was so pleased with how helpful they were. She began to see a way out.

Confronting Family Issues

Some widows' families saw them as being rich now that they had regular income. The aide could remind them that they had to support their children and could help them not to feel guilty about refusing to share their money. One widow's mother wanted her to support her sister, who had trouble keeping a job. These widows had to practice saying no.

In one instance, the aide took the widow and her small children out for ice cream, and the aide's older children came along to babysit. This did not prove satisfactory, since the two widows could not really talk. The young widow was becoming "stir crazy" because she had been reluctant to leave her children alone. The aide encouraged her to get a sitter. She found a high-school student who lived on the block to come in one afternoon a week. The children knew the girl and enjoyed being with her, and the widow could meet the aide, go shopping, or just be by herself for an hour. This plan gave the widow some space to think about herself, her feelings, and what needed doing.

The aide found one widow repainting her apartment while listening to her husband's records. The widow's sister called the aide aside and asked that she intervene. The sister believed the new widow should not work so hard and remind herself of her husband with the music. The aide had to calm the sister down and encourage her to be supportive, not critical. The new widow later explained her sister: "She couldn't understand, she's never been married."

Those widows whose husbands had died suddenly seemed to have a richer social network than those where a long illness preceded death. The illness sometimes had caused the widow to lose her ties with others:

> My husband lost all his hair and didn't want anyone to see him. People stopped coming except for the children and their husbands. When he died I couldn't simply pick up and see the people we had once known as a couple.

Not only is the illness a strain on a wife's energy, but it changes the relationship with her husband:

> He had leukemia, so for a year and a half he was back and forth for treatment. It was a big strain. I know women who have had their husbands die suddenly. It was a terrible shock for them. I don't know which is worse. Not that you're ever really prepared for it, but in one sense, even though the other is a shock, I think it is probably best [to have warning], because you know you have time to think about the idea. But still she had a healthy, normal marriage right up to the end, and I think she was lucky for that.

During their husbands' illnesses, these widows had learned to manage financially and to take charge of the household. Still, they needed help with their feelings, with how to be a widow, and with reconnecting to the world in a different way. In this all widows have the same needs. The aide knew from experience what to ask:

> I think that was one of the questions Betty asked me: "How are your in-laws?" That brought up a lot, and we discussed them for a long time. They were very possessive, old-fashioned. They were

just lost in their own self-pity. Nothing I do is right, no matter what I
try. It never is good enough. They kept acting as if the children and
I hadn't lost anything.

The aide did not always do all the helping directly, and in this
case she introduced the widow to another young widow who
lived nearby. The two had much to share, including their distress about how their in-laws reacted. It helped the new widow
to hear that the other had been disowned by her in-laws. Together they came to recognize that the problem was not in
themselves, but in their in-laws' inability to deal with the death
of their sons.

Beginning to Grieve

The aide had the perspective of experience with how grief
unfolds. She understood that the sense of disbelief protected the
new widow from her strong feelings of stress and that, as long as
this protection was in place, the widow would feel good about
how well she was doing. Sometimes she chose to wait and to be
there when things fell apart; sometimes she chose to warn the
widow:

Things may be fine now, but before they really get better they are
going to get a lot worse. I remember that once we sold my husband's business and I had a chance to stop, I fell apart.

The widow who received this warning was grateful:

It made such a difference. When I didn't think there was going to
be a tomorrow, I kept remembering what Dorothy said. I remembered she told me nothing would stay the same, that feelings don't
last forever, and that kept me going.

One widow wanted a timetable for how she would and should
be feeling. The aide tried to be reassuring but told her that there
was no fixed timetable and that everyone did things in their own
way. In effect, the message was that there is no right or wrong
way to grieve.

Denial is not impenetrable, and the widows were only partially protected from their pain. Many women had sleepless nights and found themselves weeping when they least expected it. Women who went to their physicians for help had tranquilizers prescribed, but most were uncomfortable taking them:

> I couldn't eat or sleep at first. . . . I lost a lot of weight that first winter. The doctor said I was depressed. He wanted to give me tranquilizers, but I refused. I don't believe in them. I knew this was something I had to fight and deal with.

The aide encouraged those who accepted the medications to use them for as long as they could not sleep or, in one instance, keep food down. As the widow became able to rest and keep nourishment, the aide encouraged her to taper off the number of pills and talk with the doctor about a lower dosage.

In an extreme situation, the widow had gone to her physician a few weeks after her husband died and he had referred her to a psychiatrist. The psychiatrist prescribed electroconvulsive therapy (ECT) for a reaction that, as far as the aide could tell, was a typical letdown. The widow herself felt that this treatment was not helping, but she was afraid to stop treatment. Furthermore, she did not want to offend the doctor. At the aide's insistence, she went to another physician for a second opinion. Only then, with the new doctor's prescription for a mild tranquilizer and with the specific recommendation that she did not need ECT, could she stop the treatment.

This widow's husband was an only child, and his immigrant parents were fearful that she would abandon them once she got over her acute grief. She was being pressured by them and by her husband's dying wish that she should find a new father for their children and remarry quickly. She felt guilty that she was not ready for a new relationship and that she did not necessarily want to marry the first man who offered. The conflict between her feelings, her husband's wish, and his parents' pressure was acute, and she had no experience with sorting out such conflicting demands and making decisions on her own behalf. The fact that the aide was an older woman was helpful to this widow. The aide became a kindly mother surrogate, gave her some perspective on the various issues, and made it clear that everything takes time. Later the aide referred this woman for psychological counseling; after two years the widow remarried a man whom she cared for and who enjoyed the ready-made family of her in-laws and children.

One woman, whose husband had committed suicide, had difficulty simply getting out of bed. Tension caused her to grind her teeth, and this in turn gave her a bad headache. The doctor had prescribed antidepressants, but they were not really helping. The aide could appreciate this widow's need to sleep:

> With four children, you have to get up and take care of them. She was doing that. She was not running away by sitting in barrooms all day. If sleeping is helping her, good. It's probably what she needs; it's her way of healing. The only thing I tried to discourage her from was sleeping her life away. This is something I think you have to do gradually, and I think this is why she eventually did go out and get herself a part-time job. We had been talking about it for a month.

As the widow felt her feelings legitimated, she could acknowledge the impact of the loss on her life. With the aide's support and approbation, she could begin to consider what she might do about her situation.

12 Recoil

In the recoil stage, the widow is able to experience the full pain of her grief. She cries, often at night and sometimes until she is so drained that she can cry no more. She may be troubled by disruptions in sleeping and eating patterns, by physical malaise, and by feelings of profound loneliness. The widow at this stage struggles to change the habits of daily living that had once involved her husband. She may ruminate over what she could have done to prolong her husband's life or to prevent his death. Many widows feel remorseful, guilty, or angry at this time. Not uncommonly, the widow forgets from time to time that her husband is dead or thinks she is hearing his footsteps. At the same time that she must go through all of this, family and friends may pay her less attention or may become unhelpful, as they become uncomfortable with her grief and impatient for her to return to normal. Although the stages have no set time-table, the recoil stage often begins three or four months after the death and can last for eight or nine.

Feeling Pain and Remorse

Crying has a different quality at this stage than it does when a husband has just died. Then the crying was more reflexive; now it expresses the deep sadness that comes with the full understanding of what has been lost:

> I cried a lot. I'd go to bed and after 15 minutes wake up. That didn't
> help. I guess that lasted about three months.

Sometimes a widow cries out of self-pity:

> Sometimes I feel so sorry for myself. But then I think, I have my life.
> I think of my husband and what he lost. He didn't want to die. He so
> wanted to see the kids grow up.

Crying also can reflect anxiety for the future and frustration
with the present and with the lethargy that many widows feel at
this time:

> I can't seem to get started doing anything, even cleaning the
> house. I feel so empty and lost. I think ahead and the whole thing
> feels like a black hole. Then I find myself dissolved in tears. It's like
> a vicious circle.

Instead of feeling better, the widow finds she has more
difficulty managing than when her husband first died:

> I didn't think of it as getting better. That wasn't the issue. I had
> hoped by now I would have time for all the things I wanted to do
> these past years, but I just don't feel like it.

> I had so much to do, getting rent money, getting to work, trying to
> manage. I thought I took his death very well. Then after six months
> I'd get to work and I'd start to cry—awhile every morning.

If there was an early difference between women whose husbands died suddenly and those whose husbands were ill for
some time, it disappears by now. All widows seem to have the
same letdown:

> I just seem glad to get through one day and then another. One of
> my married daughters was having a lot of problems and I didn't
> realize it. I just wasn't functioning.

In addition to the common problem of sleeplessness, some
women develop other symptoms of tension. A woman who had

trouble with grinding her teeth had to be hospitalized when her jaw locked.

The issue here is survival, not quality of life, and the widow needs to know that most widows feel this way. That in itself can help her to survive:

> Having Mary to talk to, to tell me it was normal, made it easier to survive.

Guilt, remorse, and anger come out during this period more than others. Religious faith does not comfort those who initially were angry and disillusioned by what "the Fates" had brought them. Many women talked about how they might have kept their husbands alive, like the woman whose husband was killed in an industrial accident while covering for a sick friend:

> It kept coming back over and over again. If only he hadn't gone to work that day he'd be alive. I kept asking myself, What if I had been more insistent that he stay home . . . ?

Some women used the word guilt directly:

> I felt guilty. He was trying to tell me something and I couldn't understand him. Could I have done more? The doctor wouldn't let me by his bed. I felt badly about that . . . but he said it was not going to be a peaceful death . . .

Even when a widow used the word guilt, the quality of feeling often seemed more like remorse or sadness, or perhaps anger and frustration over her impotence. Widows wanted to undo the death and to regain control over their lives. They were struggling with their powerlessness to change things and their reluctance to accept the new reality.

The widow of a man who committed suicide experienced real feelings of guilt. Before his death, she had gone to her husband's employer and to her priest for help. She described her husband's erratic behavior to them, but they put her off, belittling her concern and suggesting it was something that she was doing. After her husband did kill himself, she kept asking,

"Could I have done more?" Even with the aide there to listen and to reflect on the reality, it was two years before she could accept emotionally what she knew intellectually. She then could say to her children and mean it, "Daddy was sick; otherwise he wouldn't have done such a thing."

Another woman, the mother of two teenaged daughters, spoke of her guilt, but she seemed to use that word because she did not know how else to express what she was feeling. She was coming to realize that her life was more enjoyable without her husband. He had been a rigid man, allowing her no luxuries and barring their daughters' friends from the house. There was little laughter in their home, and he got worse when he became ill. The widow could share what she called her "secret" only because she had gotten to know the aide well enough to feel safe. The aide helped this widow to distinguish between her appropriate sadness and her competency and pleasure in her new life. The aide emphasized that the widow did not wish her husband dead, that she had been a good wife to him, and that she had fulfilled her obligations as a practicing Catholic by remaining in the marriage. She assured the widow she had no reason to feel guilty. Gradually the woman's demeanor changed as she became more relaxed and actively enjoyed her newfound self-confidence.

Over time, the widow must develop a philosophical point of view that allows her to appreciate that no one of us has control over who lives and who dies:

> We need to realize that a person's time had come. Otherwise, we would go crazy. Some people jump off a roof and survive; others are crossing the street and are suddenly dead. We have no control. A widow has to come to accept this as part of what life is about.

Confronting the Truth

Most of the recoil period involves struggling with the new reality and confronting the truth. Widows dreamed of their spouses as if they were still alive:

For months afterward I dreamed about him as if he wasn't dead.
Then I'd see him in his coffin or lying there where he died. I'd wake
up in tears. I think it took over a year before it stopped.

In spite of their wish to the contrary, widows begin to see their
husbands as dead. One widow dreamed that her husband had
come back from a trip, and in the dream she told him, "No, you
can't come in. You're not supposed to be here now." Other
women talked of setting their husband's place at the table for up
to a year and about how upset they were when they realized
what they were doing.

It was not unusual for the widow to feel her husband's
continuing presence. She might hear his car in the driveway, his
key in the door. She might find other reasons for the noise, but it
was always a great effort not to react as if he really were there:

At night as I'm lying in bed, I hear the wind blowing, and if something bangs, I think it's the door. I have all I can do to keep from
getting up to greet my husband.

One woman talked of going shopping and thinking her husband
was with her:

My husband used to drop me off first and I'd start shopping while
he parked the car. I'd wait to buy meat until he joined me. Once I
turned around and there was this man who looked like my husband, and I started to ask him what he thought of the meat I had in
my hand. I have this sign in my kitchen: "I experienced yesterday. I
am not afraid of tomorrow because I have lived today." I am trying
to get myself to believe it.

Some women avoided the bedroom for weeks, sometimes
much longer; they slept on the couch, unable to deal with the
empty place in their bed. One woman could not sleep in her
bed, even in a new house. She used the bedroom to dress in, but
still slept downstairs on the couch. She was comfortable with
this solution. Other women kept the bedroom exactly as it had
been:

The day before Dick went to the hospital he brought my breakfast to my bed. I had a cast on my leg. He went out and got a rose and put it in a vase. That vase and the rose are still alongside my bed. It's dead but it's still there. We each have our own way of getting through it.

In the presence of other widows, women would mention that they still talked to their husbands. Many were reluctant to acknowledge this until they heard that others also did it. They needed to hear from other widows that this was not unusual. One woman spoke of this in the context of her fitful sleeping:

My nights are horrible. I wake up every hour. Sometimes I talk to myself, sometimes to my husband.

Some women went on talking with their husbands for many years afterward, as they sorted out problems and tried to imagine how he would have approached them. In the earlier stages, some widows worried that this talking, their dreams, and their sense of his presence were indications that they were "going crazy." When they heard that every widow has these experiences, it tempered their concern. They could then deal more directly with the fact that their husband was really dead and with the need to change daily habits of interaction.

Coping at Different Ages

The Older Widow: Alone and No Longer Needed

Some older women alone felt an inconsolable sadness with no desire to do anything. They felt depressed and unneeded. A woman in her early sixties described her dilemma in trying to keep going despite her fatigue and depression:

No one needs me—not even my daughter. My friends aren't interested. Maybe I could get a job? How could I get a job? Maybe I could volunteer?

This widow was not ready to act; she was just beginning to explore. She sensed what she might need to do but was not yet ready to set realistic goals.

Other widows without children at home would run away from it all, if they could. One woman who worked part time stayed with her brother during the week and spent weekends with her children. She could not stand her aloneness and her loneliness. Some widows looked for a quick solution. With one act they would make things better. One woman recalled how she had ignored the aide's advice on this. She saved all her money during the first winter after her husband died and planned a trip to visit her sister in Ohio, thinking this would give her a new lease on life:

> Betty tried to warn me, but I wouldn't listen. She said, "I don't want to discourage you, but it's going to get worse. It doesn't get better." Well, I said, "It's got to get better. It couldn't be any worse than the winter nights sitting alone." So I really planned this trip, saving each week. I was more depressed on the trip. I knew I was depressed and I couldn't get out of it, and my sister didn't know what to do with me. I couldn't wait to get home.

One woman had her mother come to stay with her. Others used visits with the aide to deal with their loneliness. Some found work helpful because they did not have to dwell on themselves so much. For some, work was a "godsend," a chance to get a break, to get out.

The Widowed Mother: Parenting Alone

The young, single parent had different challenges at this time. In contrast to the older women who felt that no one needed them, women with young, dependent children were needed too much and sometimes had little to give. One woman got up each morning to get her children to school and then went back to bed to sleep away the day. Others simply withdrew. Women who both worked and cared for children often were too tired at the end of the day to do anything outside the home. Others were thinking about getting out but were concerned about who would care for their children. Some women had mothers or in-laws who could help with child care, while others got little help except what they could arrange for themselves. One woman had arranged for her child to come after school to the nursing home where she worked and to do her homework there.

The young mothers began to express concerns about their children needing a father. When children had problems, they felt inadequate. Some women emphasized the children's need for a father's companionship, and others wanted someone to discipline the children. These concerns represented a focus outside themselves, and most of these widows were able to maintain this focus and to meet their children's needs. They were eager to talk with others about how they were managing, to clarify for themselves what it meant to be a single parent, and to learn new ways of handling the many family issues. By the end of the first year, they could respond to what the children needed rather than try to protect themselves from the intrusion of the children's needs.

Seeing beyond the Family and the Old Friends

While many widows at first found their families helpful, this began to change. One young widow spoke of her family's attitude two months after the death:

> In the beginning everybody was very patient with me and now it seems that even my sisters and my mother are losing patience with me. They think that I should be over my bereavement, that I should begin to go out, that I should begin to meet gentlemen and remarry.

Some women did not feel they needed to see the aide at first because their families were so supportive. Later they were eager to talk with the aide and either reached out to her or were pleased when she called back. An older woman said her children only called her to ask her to babysit and did not think of her needs at all. Another widow said her parents were criticizing her for marrying a man who left her with no money. Another said people could not believe she felt a loss:

> Some people think I'm better off now than when he was alive. He had been drinking but for the last year he was in AA. Things were great. People don't understand the void in my life.

One widow moved in with her mother after seven months, leaving her old neighborhood and friends:

> It didn't work. My mother had no sympathy for me, and my daughter wasn't happy. Everyone kept saying find another man and get married.

Another widow said her family refused to give her any sympathy:

> My parents think that I shouldn't complain. I have the house, an income, my children. They don't see why I need pity.

Ultimately, though, sympathy or material support were not enough. The widow could feel just as alone with them as without them. The real understanding of another widow was more helpful:

> Since you are a widow, too, when you said you understood I knew you meant it and that was important. I can't stand sympathy and that's all anyone else could give me.

Widows were not prepared for their families' protective reactions, and the families' protectiveness often made the widow feel isolated:

> I feel as if everyone but Dorothy has deserted me.

For many women during this stage, the aide became a critical helper:

> There is no one else since my husband died who I can talk to like
> you.

One woman initially said, "I can't stand widows. Their talk
makes me sick." Within several months, weeping and lonely, she
called the aide. She later reported:

> I've talked to Adele about things I never said to anyone before—
> not my best friend, not my sister.

One widow reported that her family could not understand why
she needed to hear about other widows' experiences and how
they had coped:

> We can't call our families if we feel like talking about our husbands.
> They don't want to hear it. They think we'll hurt ourselves by talking
> about it.

Women whose mothers or other family members already were
widowed were able to share their common experiences with
these other widows.

Some widows had to go through several deaths. One new
widow's mother died within three months of her husband; another's widowed sister died. Both of these widows became depressed anew. Still another widow's sister committed suicide.
The burden on all of these widows was great:

> There are too many people leaning on me now since my mother
> died. I need a place where I can talk to someone who will listen to
> how I feel. Mary gives me this. I need a sense of belonging. She
> gave me moral support and self-confidence, especially when I
> needed to look for a more suitable job.

The need for the understanding of friends became critical
as widows began to feel like going out again. They dreaded
coming home to an empty house so much that it sometimes
seemed better not to go out at all. As one woman said, it was like
going to a party and then having no one with whom to share the
experience. Just when they were ready for friends again, the

widows found their old friends unhelpful and felt left out or
misunderstood by their married friends:

> You have the feeling that, no matter where you go and no matter
> what, you are an extra. At a wedding not long ago a neighbor said
> there were just 10 of us so we could all sit together. She forgot
> about me. I was the eleventh. I could have screamed.

> With married friends, they don't understand what it means to be a
> widow. They talk about their husbands without even realizing it . . .

Married friends often stopped calling, and even when they kept
in touch, the widow often found their company less than satisfactory:

> We went to a play. I wanted to tell them how much I thought my
> husband would have enjoyed it. I knew no one wanted to hear that.
> Then we got into a hassle about paying for dinner.

Within the first year, some women were beginning to look
for new social connections. They recognized that their old social
networks were inadequate:

> I really didn't have too many friends. I was wrapped up in my
> husband and children and didn't have girlfriends like so many
> others have.

> I need someone to talk to, someplace to go where I will be
> accepted. No one rings my doorbell any more. My old friends have
> left me. I need new friends.

> Weekends were awful. I needed new people in my life, friends who
> wanted to do things together. We needed something in common,
> but we also needed to be able to hear each other. I wanted friends
> who would understand if I talked about being lonely or about going
> back to work.

A year after her husband's death, one woman reported
feeling depressed, tired, and lonely. She thought she was visiting
her husband's grave too often, she heard him walking in the
house, and she said she was "desperate to get out." Some

women talked about "breaking out of the solitude," and others said simply, "I need to get away from the four walls." One woman, who initially was reluctant to get involved with the program, told her daughter, "I don't care what kind of a racket it is. I need to get out."

Helping Them Get Out and Make Friends

Since the aide could never have satisfied the widows' needs for friendship, she would arrange for them to meet each other at small social gatherings or invite them to the program's more formal meetings which included cookouts, discussion groups, and informal living-room get-togethers. In addition, several church groups in the area sponsored social clubs for the widowed. Some aides regularly attended club meetings and invited the new widows to go with them.

Some widows were naturally shy and needed much encouragement. The aide sometimes would have to work hard just to get them to join her and some other widows at a movie. These efforts often paid off, though, as in one aide's description of a homebody in her late fifties:

> I had to call her many times before she agreed to come. She finally made it when I agreed to pick her up. She had a good time and promised that next time she would get there on her own. She even took two phone numbers to call other women she met.

Having the company of other widows seemed to make a difference for these reticent women. One widow, whom the aide had not yet met, appeared in response to a cookout invitation. She had not come to any earlier activities, but now that her needs were changing she was curious about what would go on. She was pleased with what she found, as were most widows:

> It was very reassuring. I wasn't a fifth wheel and I felt that I belonged.

> It was helpful to share my feelings. Everyone was friendly and willing to listen.

One widow who had been physically ill looked so much better and happier that her doctor asked if she had been to Florida for a holiday:

> I told him simply I had met a group of widows and found out my problems were not unusual. Everyone has the same difficulties. It made me feel better. I plan to go to everything from now on.

The aide also would arrange meetings between two women she thought would be compatible and helpful to each other. Here are two examples:

> Betty gave me the name of this widow. She was young like myself. She had three young children and as a result I had more in common with her than with Betty. She had lost her husband about a year and a half before mine. She was still having a hard time, but she helped me a lot. We used to call each other at 11:30 at night and talk until 1:00 A.M. She was the same way. She would just sit and talk.

> We lived within two blocks of each other. If Dorothy hadn't introduced us, we'd have never met. My house is so empty now. It made me feel good to help someone else.

Sometimes the two widows were neighbors and could look out for each other:

> I'll keep an eye out for her. When I see the light on, I'll drop in.

These encounters not only began to fill social needs, but they also made the widow feel needed again. She now had something special to offer to others.

Moving toward Accommodation

Sharing the Truth

The company of other widows seemed to make a difference in widows' ability to talk about their husbands, though timing was important and some women came to the group activities too soon. Since they could not yet identify themselves as widows, they found the talk about grief and widowhood too depressing.

Some of those women who were not ready to talk about their husbands as dead would protect themselves with such expressions as "He is away," or "Before he left." One aide found the right moment to help a widow move beyond this pattern:

> I suddenly realized as we were talking together that Ruth talked about her husband as if he were on vacation. She never used the word dead. I finally said to her, "You know he's dead. He's not coming back." By then she was ready to hear me. We hugged each other and she smiled. It wasn't a smile of joy, but more of recognition. She said, "I guess I can't keep running can I?" It's funny. I hadn't really thought this through. It just felt right to say it. But afterward she started to talk about going to work and what she could do with herself. She'd been avoiding that too.

The aide's initiative could have misfired if it had not been in the context of a relationship between two widows who knew each other well and understood each other's pain. The aide's intervention worked because she had a good sense of timing and knew she would be heard.

Women were ready to come to gatherings with other widows when they no longer had trouble identifying themselves as widows:

> I began to realize that I would not be here [at this meeting] if I were not a widow too.

At this point, they were ready to talk not only about how their husbands had lived, for example, his likes and dislikes, but they also could ask each other, "How did your husband die?" For this they needed to feel safe:

> I was really ready to get out of my box, but I needed to feel safe, to be sure that I would be accepted and that if I wanted to talk about my husband it would be all right.

The supportive environment of the widows' group was especially important to the widow of a man who had committed suicide. She could not tell most people the truth about his death. If she did, people would pull back in horror, their unspoken message being, "What did you do?" Her children were teased in their old neighborhood, and when they moved to a new neighborhood she told people he had had a heart attack. She lived in terror that the "family secret" would come out, and she did not know how to deal with the criticism implicit in people's reactions to the truth. The aide encouraged her to separate herself from her husband's problems and helped her to confront her feelings of shame, with the goal of freeing her from her secrets. This widow had an invaluable encounter at one of the program's gatherings, recounted by one of the aides:

> She was always worried about people reacting with, "What did you do that led to this?" People are like that. I kept telling her that she didn't have to think that way about herself. Her family had a lot of problems and they never let her feel good about herself. Her mother-in-law actually did blame her for ignoring her son's long-term problems. I finally got her to come to the cookout by bringing her. Sure enough, she sat next to Wilma, who I knew would ask and she did. Joan later came up to me looking very pleased. She told me what happened. She had simply answered, "He committed suicide." She couldn't believe it when all she got back was, "You must feel awful—how are you doing?" It opened a new door for her to see that people were concerned and listened.

Becoming More Independent

Many women did not drive and had depended on their husbands to take them visiting or to do chores outside the neighborhood. With the aide's encouragement, several widows learned to drive and make use of the family car. Once they were mobile, they could be more independent, and this pleased both them and the aides:

> Tomorrow night is the first widows' meeting at the Espousal. One of the widows is coming with me. I called her the other day. Since her husband died she has learned how to drive. They had a car and she never drove. I had told her it was crazy to have a car and not drive. Last spring she started to take lessons. When I called to

invite her, I offered to pick her up. She said, "No, I have a license. I'll meet you at your house." She was as pleased as could be. This was a whole new thing for her.

Driving or sharing rides with a neighbor was also a key to holding a job:

Dee is trying to get me to go with her to get a part-time job. She figures we can get a job someplace together and she would drive.

Not only did widows make new friends, but they also shared resources. Some women had to learn about developing these resources. One widow who called the aide for everything gradually accepted the need to find another widowed friend. She relaxed and became more receptive to opportunities around her, but she needed almost the same encouragement a child needs from a mother when moving out for the first time. She had to recognize that, as much as she needed, she also had much to give.

This same widow also put considerable energy into meeting another man. Like other widows at this stage, she was not yet ready for real involvement in a new relationship, but she saw this as the only way out of her pain and loneliness. After this woman had been widowed for about nine months, she had a slump. Like a young teenager, she was upset because a man she had met did not call as he had promised. An aide explained:

I guess the man did not call her, the weather was getting bad, and she does not have enough to do. She does not work full time, and just being alone in the house is not doing the right thing. They feel she should go out and circulate more and not just with men. Her brother finally bought her a secondhand car. I said that will be wonderful, because if you are lonely you can pick up and go someplace, to visit or to shop. The problem is that she really needs someone there constantly to tell her what to do. I don't think that she has ever made a decision alone since the time she was married 25 years ago.

This widow's family was supportive and appropriately helpful, and they could not be the focus of her discontent. She needed self-confidence and a sense of her own competency. The aide could help her by going places with her or by reviewing in detail how to handle a new situation. She had to clarify, however, that her purpose was to help the widow learn to manage by herself and to feel pleased about her ability to do so.

The new widow must learn that she sometimes will have a slump and feel depressed and that this is all right. Little by little, she will begin to make the moves that will give her life new perspective and that will direct her toward an accommodation. Being with other widows can be a valuable asset along the way:

> When I saw all those other women making a good adjustment, I decided I had to pull myself together.

> I realized that I was not the only one to whom this happened, and that helped me get going again.

Seeing other widows gives the widow role models and choices, as explained by one widow whose husband had been dead about a year and a half:

> I kept thinking of myself as helpless. Every time someone asked me to do something for another widow, I said, "No, I can't do that." I was really getting more and more into a hole. I looked around me and thought that I could die, like the widow up the street [an 80-year-old woman] who died right after her husband died. I realized that I did not want to go that way. Then I looked at Dorothy [the aide], and I saw I had a choice. I could be like her and that seemed like the way I wanted it to be. It was my choice. I felt like an alcoholic. They say you have to hit bottom before the change. I guess I did crash, but when I was ready to get up there was someone there to show me the way.

13 Accommodation

The widow begins to reach accommodation when she first understands what she must do in order to turn from the past to the future. She begins to recognize that her bereavement as such will never end and that she still will feel pain and sadness from time to time. At this stage, she sees that for life to continue she must make basic changes in how she sees herself and how she lives her life. She accepts the fact that things will never be the same and that she herself will be changed by the experience. Eventually, she finds a new sense of self and self-confidence, she feels better, and she understands how she has changed:

> I have to keep fighting the family image of me as the "village idiot." I was the baby and they never believed I could do anything. They always said, "Don't tell her, she'll forget. She doesn't know how to do anything." Here I am standing on my own two feet, taking care of my children. I have to remind them that I am doing it. I've taken responsibility that I never had before. I didn't need to before but now I'm doing it, and I'm proud of myself.

Turning to the Future

The widow at this point has begun to see herself in roles other than that of wife and has her sights set on the future. She will continue to grow, to develop, and to cope with a life that has a different dynamic now that she is single.

179

A widow begins to make all these changes when she can say, "I am a widow." At the same time, she may always harbor some sense of disbelief:

> There are times when I need to see the grave marker. When I am with other couples, then it hits me that he's really gone. It is still hard to believe, and I guess I will always feel that way.

She can accept her feelings, her occasional pain, and her situation. She begins to understand that you never finish mourning as such, and children are constant reminders:

> I think that they are growing up to be . . . well, I think he would be very proud of them, and that's what really hurts. Like when my daughter learned to dive and my son to swim. These are things that you'll never get over, because then it will be graduation and their weddings. You know there is no replacement. Even a step-father is not their father. You can't replace people.

Even without the children as a reminder, a widow keeps on mourning:

> I don't think that you ever finish mourning. I mean you don't brood; there's a difference. But as far as mourning the person, you mourn them the rest of your life. You reminisce, but you don't brood or dwell on the past. I think you have to learn to look ahead a little to the future. I used to feel such self-pity. Why was I picked on? You have to pick up the pieces. I just don't know how or when—but somehow I overcame these things.

For some widows, turning to the future is an act of will. Others do it more gradually as they become aware of and respond to the resources for coping with their new needs. They can act more out of deliberation and less out of desperation, and they actively change their relationships to the past:

> You begin to realize that tears won't bring him back. You can miss him and there's many a night that I hug the pillow and say "Oh, I want you so bad." But you can't bring him back, so there's no

sense in crying. You've got to make a life for yourself. You have to go on, and you just have to make the best of it and accept life as it is.

You just can't live on grief forever. If you do you'll find yourself cutting paper dolls or something else. I had a long road to walk before I felt that maybe I could face the world. All of a sudden it dawns on you, that if I don't go out and really work I'm not going to have a roof. . . . You have to face the world in a way that you did not before, because a wife working is in cooperation with her husband, for the extras. Now it's for real.

They are aware of their needs and their responsibilities to themselves, and they begin to think of how they will deal with the rest of their lives, now that they are alone:

I have a few years until I get Social Security. When I realized that my husband lost his pension by several months and I lost the benefits as his widow, I knew I had to get a job where there was security. I could get more money elsewhere, but the telephone company had good benefits. I have to think about that now, so I'm staying.

For me the hardest thing to get used to now is budgeting. My husband always used to take care of the household. I had freedom with whatever I earned on my own. Now I have to live within my means. I have some insurance money, but still I have to think ahead. You have to have some savings. Rents are going up and God forbid if I ever got sick!

Assuming New Roles

The widow starts moving away from the daily activities that tied her to her husband and to her role as his wife:

I have reorganized my day so I am not waiting at home for him at 4:30. I try to get out for lunch at a nice restaurant. I may do a little shopping to distract myself. When I get home I feel satisfied to settle in and watch TV. The neighborhood isn't safe, and I don't like to go out at night. I used to enjoy knitting, but I find that boring. I think I will get a part-time job to meet people, even though I don't need the money.

This woman needed new activities to replace the ones she had given up, and the aide told her about the center for adult education where she might take classes in crafts and meet people as well. She became interested and appreciated the aide's suggestion.

Another widow who was very involved with her husband in church and community activities sought a new community:

I was always his wife. I needed to find a new community. It is difficult to make new friends. I hate to go alone, but I do. I have found another church where no one knew me. I've become very involved and so have the children, and I have made new friends. Maybe it is better to call them special acquaintances at this point.

One widow, whose husband had had a drinking problem, had joined Al-Anon when he joined AA. For 18 months after his death she kept going to the meetings. Finally she decided to stop:

Drinking was his problem, not mine. I don't want to go to those meetings any more. That's not where I'm at now.

Some widows could not reorder their lives and move away from being their husbands' wives. One widow would go to lunch with friends during the day, as she had done when her husband was alive. Weekends and evenings she would call the aide to complain about her loneliness and despair and about her children not staying home when she needed them. Even though it was against her own well-being, she kept herself as her husband had wished. About the possibility of working, she insisted, "He didn't want me to work and I won't work now." This woman lived as her husband's wife, despite her changing situation, and she would not make any accommodation that confronted her with her widowhood.

Many other women at this stage do not even think of themselves as widows any more. A woman whose husband had been dead for two and a half years found a different way to describe herself:

> I used to think of myself as a widow for a long time. I seem to be through with that now. I'm not sure I have a good word. I'm single, I guess, a formerly married, single parent.

Another woman, also a single parent, took up sewing lessons at a community center and supported her new identity by participating in group discussions about being a single parent.

As children grow older, the widow's involvement in parenting changes, and older mothers begin to worry about being too dependent on their adult children.

> My children are good to me. I'm looking forward to being a grandmother. That will give me pleasure. The hardest time is the loneliness. I seem to have lost a lot of incentive, but I am moving ahead. I'm learning to drive, although I never wanted to. I didn't want to work, but now I have to. I'm learning to stand on my own two feet. The kids have their own lives. I have to find friends to do things with on weekends. I was so grateful when Mary told me about the programs at Arch Street.

Grown children can be a comfort, but they also have their own lives to live:

> I have to show the children that I can be independent. They have their own lives. I'm too young to let them think they have to take care of me.

For their part, the children reacted in a variety of ways. Some were responsive and respectful of their mother's needs, and others continued a pattern of taking from her all the time. One widow said her son wanted her to sell her home so that she could give him his share of the inheritance. She had to know her own needs and learn to set limits:

> I always thought of the children first, but now I know I have to think of my own needs and my future. I'm alone, and all I have is what I earn and the house.

Widows with young children had to think about what they would do once the children went off to school or had grown up. Some widows initiated this discussion themselves, and others required some prompting from the aide. Some of these widows still needed to finish high school, and others needed vocational counseling. Several started night school, and others looked for part-time work while the children were at school. These widows had to accept themselves in the new role as the family's prime breadwinner, a role they never before had considered for themselves.

Associated with developing new roles and a new sense of independence is the capacity to make decisions. One woman was amazed that she had the ability to make major decisions:

> I never believed I could have done it, but I found this house. I looked over my money and decided to buy it. It was a smart move to a better neighborhood, better schools, and closer to my family.

This woman found a new sense of self-confidence in her success with decisions. A widow with grown children also valued her new self-confidence:

> I have everything I want. I work. I think it gives you a little self-confidence in yourself. I think that confidence is the most important thing of all. If you have confidence in yourself, you can get by with anything. I enjoy my home and I try to enjoy myself.

Discovering Inner Strength

Most women who had struggled to understand their husbands' untimely deaths eventually recognized that they could not undo the facts. Many others who once had been devout lost their faith at first but at this stage rediscovered meaning in their faith:

It was the benevolent hand of God. A half-hour sooner when we were all in the car, and we would have all died.

My husband was a minister. He loved the church. His one idea was to make heaven his home. I feel that's where he is now. At the beginning that didn't help. Now it helps me a lot to think of him there. He's in a better place.

Religion could sustain a widow through the low points:

My faith makes a real difference for me. You need that kind of belief to keep going.

Accommodation does not mean an absence of problems, and not all problems are the result of widowhood. A pervasive problem that is a result of being widowed is loneliness:

We were always together. I'm glad to be at work. I'm more friendly with the people there now. I'm making new friends.

Some women were comforted in loneliness by the memory of their husbands:

I get lonesome, especially at night when the kids are gone. If I can't sleep I just take a bus sometimes and go up to the cemetery. I sit there and talk to myself. One day last winter it was cold and windy. It felt good to walk up there and stand in the wind. I came home and I felt much better.

Driving gave many widows a new sense of personal freedom and strength. One woman, against all advice, sold her car and could not afford to buy a new one; she felt trapped. Other women learned to drive for the first time:

It's good to have a car, even to get away from everything or just to take a little drive, to see something different when you get uptight about something at home. I live near the beach. I very often just get in the car and drive over there. There's something about the water. I just look at it and it sort of relaxes me. Then I come back and I can face things.

The widow finds strength in new relationships and activities and also within herself:

> If I am lonely I can call up two or three people now. There is always someone to go to the movies with, or to just talk.

> I would never have done this before, but a neighbor called to come to a survey she was doing for a cereal company. I had such a good time. The kids teased me when I boasted that I earned seven dollars. We're not going to buy a stereo with that kind of money. We all enjoyed my pleasure in getting out and doing something different. You'd be surprised how it changed my attitude.

> I found out there were things I thought I could never do and I am doing them. It's a very good feeling. I don't even mind being alone. I used to be afraid of that. It is better now. It's my choice. I can choose when I want to be alone.

The change can be dramatic, as one aide recalled:

> She had such a hard, closed-in expression. She was negative about everything. I met her at the meeting the other night. I guess her husband must be dead about two and a half years now. She looked stunning. The best-looking woman in the crowd. She was talking to people, reaching out. Her whole manner was changed.

Of herself this same widow said, "I am more involved and more outgoing than I ever was, even before my husband died."

Choosing an Intimate Lifestyle

New friends and social roles will never replace the intimacy of a marital relationship:

> No one else cares what the children said. It was only important to the two of us. There is no one to complain to, to share the small things with. But mostly I miss being cherished. It really was a 50-50 marriage, long before women's liberation. It was more than love. We cherished and cared for each other. He used to leave my

birthday card in out-of-the-way places. My son does the same thing. We can't afford big things, but he knew how to make me feel good. I really miss that and I know that I won't have it again. I am happy for the fact that I did have it, and that is very important to me.

One way out of loneliness is to remarry, but not all widows wanted this:

I never want to be tied down by marriage again. When I want to go out now, I can go. My life is really my own. I find that I have this freedom. If I have a chance to go out to dinner with the girls at the office, I do, and I enjoy it. This is not just sour grapes. We had a good life together, but now I think it is time to be alone. Maybe later I'll change my mind.

Others saw remarriage as a good possibility:

I think if anyone has a chance to remarry, then they should. While my children are single I will never marry, but after they are married that's different. You can't live your life for them and they can't live yours. If I found someone that's nice, with enough money so that we won't be destitute, then I'd have someone for a companion.

Widows talked about the need for love, respect, and financial security in a marriage. Women who had had good marriages were more willing to consider that they might remarry. Some believed there was only one man for them. Regardless of whether they contemplated remarriage, all widows felt that they could manage alone in a way that they never before had considered possible.

As time went by, some women began to talk about the problems in their marriages. Many more men than initially was apparent had had drinking problems, and this influenced how a widow felt about remarriage:

I miss him very much. We had lots of good times. But he did drink and we lost out on lots of chances to get ahead because of it. In some ways it is better now—although I wouldn't admit it to my family. I don't think I want to take a chance on marriage again.

Older Catholic women seemed generally more accepting of their fate and their loneliness. They did not actively seek male companionship that might lead to remarriage:

I'm satisfied with my family and my friends and my children.

Jewish women more often wanted social outlets where they could meet men, and they more often considered remarriage.

As the widows began to meet men and to start dating, other problems arose. The aide could talk with them (whatever their age or religious background) about dating as adults. None of these women had dated since they were teenagers, and they brought old habits and expectations to the dating scene. When they became more comfortable with themselves and more confident about their ability to deal with the world, they could relax and accept the fact that remarriage is only one solution.

Most women felt clearly ambivalent about dating and remarriage. One woman was very clear that she did not want to remarry but talked with excitement about a friend arranging a date with a widower. Widows needed to learn that they could date and enjoy male companionship and not necessarily have any greater intimacy with the man or consider marrying him:

A man at work seemed inclined to go out with me, but I was disgusted when I sensed that all he wanted was sex. All I wanted was some good companionship, and certainly no sex outside of marriage.

The aide counseled a widow that, before she remarries, a woman should know she can manage alone:

I was grateful for Adele talking to me like that. I was acting as if I was 16 years old again. That was the last time I had a date. I would sit by the phone and wait. I was so afraid to be alone. But I didn't need that pressure, as if being married was everything. I needed to learn that I didn't need a man to take care of me. Now maybe I am ready to get married if I meet someone I really like.

In-laws were often a problem when a widow began to date:

The first time I dated I felt guilty. I was sure my husband would find out—as if I was cheating. Then my in-laws started on me about being disloyal to his memory. I don't know if they thought that I should sit home in black all the time. Mary was really great in helping me understand my own feelings, and that it was all right to enjoy myself. She also helped me see that I had to live my life and that I would never be able to please my in-laws. At least now I don't fight with them.

One young widow met someone she wanted to marry, and her children were eager for this. They were too young to remember their father and they wanted a father. She had not planned to remarry and did not want to marry simply to fill her loneliness. She talked for hours with the aide, wanting to be sure that she cared for the man in his own right. As a practicing Catholic, she could not afford to make a mistake. She also needed support in dealing with her dead husband's parents, who were afraid the children would not remember their father. Her own parents were most supportive. She was finally comfortable with her decision to remarry:

When we did marry, I knew I loved this man who would be a good father to my children. I really looked forward to having his children as well. He's understanding of my in-laws' feelings. If they can accept him, he wants them to feel welcome. I just know that we can work it out for us.

Widows talked all these matters over with each other as well as the aide. Eventually, as they developed relationships with each other, moved away from their grief, and looked to the future, the aide became less important in their lives.

Several social groups for single adults were organized at about this time. Women who became involved in these groups invested much energy in them, and the groups became important sources of approbation. A woman with organizational talent was elected president of one group. At this time, widows did not want to join sectarian groups. They were moving away from their grief and expanding their social networks, and they sought people with whom they would have more in common than their faith. They looked for people with common interests, views, and outlooks about life.

Some women no longer found comfort in all-female company. These women eventually stopped their involvement in widow groups, not because they wanted remarriage, but because they did not consider movies or dinner out a good time. They wanted something more active and more distracting:

> I like to dance. I want to find male companionship and have a good time. I don't want to be with other widows. They talk about their problems, and that is depressing.

Some younger women expressed concern about spending so much time with other widows:

> I can't make this my whole life. I have to find other interests and other things.

The aide encouraged this woman to maintain the friendships she had made but to find new activities for herself. For older women, the friendships with widows and the widowed organizations were central in their lives:

> I'd be lost without some of these activities. I'm going to Florida with a group this winter, and last year I went to Ireland. I had always wanted to travel and I thought I would never have the chance once my husband died. We have a good time together—just the women. I'm not saying that it's all a bed of roses, but at least I am enjoying things and doing things I never thought I'd do.

By this time, the future no longer seemed so bleak.

> I don't think much about the past any more. There were good things that I miss, but there are good things now. I'm too involved to dwell on the past.

14 Widowhood and Mutual Help

This chapter summarizes the evidence for mutual help as the most potent approach to helping women cope with bereavement, grief, and widowhood. Data from the Widow-to-Widow project and some new concepts based on these data constitute the foundation for discussion of the organization of help, the focus of help, and the process of helping via "linking relationships."

The Organization of Help

The Value of Outreach

The Widow-to-Widow project not only provided assistance in the form of mutual-help experiences but did so without waiting for the widowed participants to ask for assistance. Universal outreach to whole cohorts of people who might need help departs radically from the way help is usually made available in Western societies. Where autonomy and independence are cherished virtues, we traditionally have believed it appropriate to wait until people ask for help. Friends will avoid intruding on a bereaved or troubled friend. "Call me if you need something," they will say, instead of keeping in touch to find out if the person really does need something. Professional helpers and systems of help generally will assist a person in response to a person's request. The person's request signifies to the professional people that the person truly wants assistance. Professional people in the mental health field go even farther in their expectations, evaluating the person's request in order to determine whether that individual truly wants to do something about the current difficulty, that is, whether the person has the requisite "motivation" to change and hence deserves help. The burden throughout our society falls on the individuals in need—to know what they need, to figure out from whom they can receive assistance, and even to demonstrate that they want and will use the help.

In the Widow-to-Widow program, we set out to disregard these conventions of friendship and professionalism. The project reached out to every member of the target population. A significant number of women responded favorably to the outreach, a simple offer of assistance, repeated periodically in different ways. These women did not feel the offer was either inappropriate or intrusive. The women's acceptance of help did not mean they had no other ties or available help. Most women were involved actively with children and other nearby family. Over time, though, the nearby (and generally once-helpful) relatives grew unsympathetic and impatient. Rather than helping the widow, they undermined her efforts to help herself. Since they wanted her to be done with her mourning, they were unable to help her onward as she needed. Widows welcomed the program's open-ended offer of help when it came because they felt they could not say just what their specific needs were, nor could they organize themselves to find other appropriate services. Mothers at home with dependent children accepted almost immediately. Suddenly confronting the needs of their children and the responsibilities of single parenthood, they wanted guidance in understanding their children's feelings and reactions to their father's death. Most of all these mothers needed something for themselves. (Working women were less likely to accept in the early stage of widowhood.)

Typical of most new widows, many women reflected both their family's wishes and our society's values in wanting to appear independent and able to manage on their own. Because of this, a few widows did flounder for a time until they could talk with the aide or spend any time with her. Because the offer came to them, though, most new widows did not see their integrity being compromised. Indeed, the outreach gesture made clear to them that they did not have to manage alone or prove to themselves or others that they had no needs they could not meet themselves.

The Value of Peers as Helpers

Because the person reaching out was another widow who came to call informally, the new widow felt herself in the positive role of a neighbor in need of temporary assistance. Just when others were pulling away, the aide brought friendship and understanding. The widow's only obligation was optional. If she chose, she could reciprocate when and if she was ready.

Had this help been offered by any professional person, except perhaps by a member of the clergy, the new widow would have found herself in the position of being someone with a deficit, someone who needed treatment to make her whole. At a time when a woman is already feeling weak and disabled, becoming a professional person's client or patient simply reinforces her sense of inadequacy and defectiveness. Too often she enters yet another experience in which she discovers that she is not in full control of her own life.

I do not intend here to degrade professional help but rather to suggest that other types of help may be more effective in certain circumstances. I have three concerns about professional help in the circumstances of bereavement. First, professional people and their agencies are products of their societies and so reflect many of the values and attitudes of their communities, including the values and attitudes about death. Regardless of the recent educational emphasis on death and dying, most professional people still have difficulty coping with grief and understanding the profound disruptions brought on by death. Of at least equal importance is the culture of professional help itself. Treatment and professional help imply underlying deficiency, disease, or dysfunction. When bereavement and grief become the targets of therapies, they take on the image of aberrations to be exorcised. Grief and bereavement are more properly seen as elemental human experiences. My final concern pertains to the professional concept of expertise. Institutions for caring tend to honor professional expertise and to segregate people from each other, routinizing human interactions around professional experts. Organized in this way, they are remote from the social context and the experiential learning that foster personal growth. The Widow-to-Widow program organized itself around the needs that people have for each other and the value of sharing the expertise that laypeople gain from the experience of living.

Emphasis on Learning

Most widows in our society have no special place where they can learn to be widows or where their problems are articulated in terms of transitions and learning. The relationship between adaptation and learning is reciprocal. As White (1974) pointed out, all adaptation involves learning, and people's learning opportunities affect their adaptive strategies. A mutual-help organization is one of the few places in our society where people can learn how to adapt to a critical transition. Because of its emphasis on mutualism and its lay orientation, the group does not have to wait for prospective participants to apply. Members can reach out as friends and neighbors. The member reaching out has the special qualities of a peer who is an insider, someone who lives every day with similar circumstances. The learning offered does not come from a clinical sample or from a book, but from a fellow traveler's life experience. The source of learning has a singular value, as one widow in the program reflected:

> I wish there had been something like this when my mother was widowed. She had six small children. She had a nervous break-down. She couldn't face it alone. My aunt came and took care of us for a year. My mother couldn't talk to her, as she'd never been married. None of her friends were widowed.

The form of the offer also seems especially suitable. A person who is grieving or making adaptations over time may not learn on anyone else's schedule or during someone's time-limited sessions. Mutual help means a person will be there for another person, when and if the other wants help:

> She did that for—well, it will be four years since my husband died. She would call and say, "How are you?" I would think that she was calling for just a few minutes, but then we would just talk and she would get me to let my trouble out. I always felt so much better afterwards. Sometimes I would carry her number around with me. It made me feel better to know that she was there if I needed her.

The learning opportunities created by a mutual-help organization, while open-ended in form, stem from the concrete experiences of others. The information arises from the interpersonal setting and is therefore immediately relevant and accurate. In their list of information that people seek in new circumstances, Hamburg and Adams (1967) emphasize the importance of information about the circumstance, about the personal experience of such a circumstance, and about ways of dealing with the difficulty. The widowed helper is an expert at conveying such information to another widow. Sometimes the information that widows seek is specific, and at other times it is more contextual, such as how to be confident in going ahead or whether the direction and the process are right or wrong:

> Dorothy always made me feel that whatever works for you is all right. She gave me confidence that it was all right to use trial and error to find a way.

Such information is digested and assimilated more easily when the people exchanging it have the special relationship that comes from having experienced similar difficulties:

> The aide's help was different because she had been there. She knew the pain. She had told me what to expect.

> I could talk to my mother when she was alive because she was widowed. I could talk to the aide because she was widowed. When my mother died, I had to call Betty. There was no one else I could talk to.

Emphasis on Linking Relationships

A mutual-help model may be particularly suitable for meeting women's needs, since it is at base a relational model and usually offers further learning and growth opportunities through the medium of "linking relationships." A linking relationship is one that helps a person to bridge the gap between one phase of life and the next. In the Widow-to-Widow program, the widows' relationships with other widows were the primary means of facilitating their transitional process. Through these linking relationships, the new widow saw options for herself and learned to cope more effectively with change.

Most women experience resistance to assuming the role of widow, not simply because they are reluctant to let go of the wife role, but because they share with the rest of society a negative view of the widow role. With the widow role comes both an image of death and the implication that a woman is no longer complete. Thus, the linking relationships neither replace past relationships nor create new dependencies. New dependencies only would reinforce the negative sense of self the widow experiences. Instead, the new widow is involved in a transitional relationship that supplies her with support and assistance for negotiating her transition. With the widowed helper, she enters into a mutual interdependency typical of the nonhierarchical relationship between peers or siblings.

The Focus of Help for Widows

Illness Prevention or Coping Assistance?

The Widow-to-Widow program was intended in part as a preventive intervention for helping widows to avoid developing serious psychiatric illness consequent to bereavement. In fact, very few widows ever seemed in danger of developing serious emotional illness. Those who showed this risk typically had preexisting illnesses and were already receiving professional help.

Widows of all ages felt some distress over relationships in their lives, and they lacked knowledge about making new friends. Older women were more likely to be alone and in need of companionship. Younger women longed for time alone away from the children, and they needed people with whom they could talk about feelings and pressures. Many found work a meaningful outlet where they could be involved with others. Work was also a place where another sense of self remained intact. As working women aged, however, they could not ignore the question of what would happen to them when they could work no longer. If work was a place where they were connected with other people, they had to find a way to meet this need outside of the work place.

Older women often were preoccupied with health worries. They feared that with increasing age they would not be able to manage alone and that they would not have enough money to care for themselves when they were no longer able to work. Most women needed to feel needed and sought continuity in the caretaking roles they had as wives. The role of mother, even with adult children, was still available to them.

For many of these women, the Widow-to-Widow program led to a permanent network of new friends with whom they could share their lives. For younger women, the association with other widows was in response to a temporary need while they grieved and until they eventually relinquished the role of wife.

To return to the matter of outcome and illness prevention, I cannot say that the program prevented any new illnesses from developing. Most widows did have serious problems over an extended period of time, some more extreme than others, and they seemed to learn through their involvement with the program how to cope more effectively with these problems. They were not without problems at the end of the project; they simply seemed better able to manage themselves and their lives. After all, life is ongoing, and so are outcomes. The program was successful to the extent that it helped people through times of distress; showed them they could carry on with some joy, pleasure, and excitement; and supported them as they met the problems of daily living with a somewhat different point of view.

Basic Needs for Help

A main product of the Widow-to-Widow project was the information we gathered about the problems that new widows confront in their lives and how they manage their problems over
time. We also gained new knowledge about how the death of a
husband affects a woman and what kinds of help she needs and
values.

The new widow must cope with two fundamental issues.
First, she must deal with her feelings of sadness, despair, and
aloneness, the feelings that are typically associated with grief.
She must accept both the feelings and the associated pain with
the understanding that they are expectable, natural, and appropriate. Second, she must confront the inner and outer
changes that are the inevitable consequences of loss. The widow's loss requires that she reorient most of her life patterns and
many of its meanings. In her everyday life, she no longer can
play the role of wife to her husband. She eventually must give
up this role and the meanings it has conferred upon her individuality. In the course of this, she temporarily dons the role of
widow. Ultimately, she moves away from the widow role and
its meanings and learns to think of herself as a woman who was
formerly married, a woman who is now single, and who has
found new sources of meaning in her life. Making these transitions, a woman in effect changes her sense of who she is. She
develops a new identity and finds a new sense of self. The
assistance she is given must be responsive, usually in sequential
fashion, both to her painful feelings and to her critical life
transition.

These findings from the outreach program are corrobo-
rated by data about those who called the Widowed Service
Line. There is an interesting contrast between the needs of the
callers and those who were offered the person-to-person help of
the outreach program. This contrast lies in the time that had
elapsed since bereavement, during which widows struggled to
achieve an accommodation to their loss. Five and six years after
the death, many callers to the Widowed Service Line were
talking about its meaning for the first time. Many expressed the
wish that there had been an outreach program when they were

first widowed and remarked that for the first time they had found a place where someone would listen to them. Newly widowed callers, like the newly widowed in the outreach program, were confronting their painful feelings and having difficulty acknowledging their loss, and they talked about others not understanding them. Many of the new widows who called, a larger percentage than would be represented in a widowed population in general, had young children at home. Most callers who had been widowed two or three years were then seeking ways to reengage in the social system in new ways, and they were looking for help to build a new life and to make new friends. Callers were grateful that help targeted to their special needs was being advertised widely and was so readily available, and they especially valued the help of another widow.

Linking Relationships throughout the Stages of Transition

Just as the recent psychological research suggests that a woman's definition of self evolves from her connectedness with and caring about others, I would suggest a corollary for the woman in transition. Before a woman can relinquish her prior connections, she may need to develop new relationships that link her to others. A shift in identity will emerge from these linking relationships and will also lead to new relationships that are appropriate to her redefinition of herself and to her changed life situation.

As she makes the transition from wife to widow, the new widow has the opportunity to make a major shift in how she sees herself and how she relates to others. She begins to find a new way of evaluating her connectedness to others and her need for others. From the opportunity created by her widowhood, she may shift her whole process of self-definition. She may become less embedded and less dependent on her relationships for defining who she is. She also may free her sense of self from any one role she plays. When she loses the wife role, she feels a loss of self and of her place in the whole order of things. As she learns to disengage her own sense of worth and adequacy from this one role, she may learn to invest her self-definition less in any other current or future role. In the role of widow, she no longer will accept society's judgment that she is the author of her own misfortune and no longer will turn inward, feeling trapped, helpless, and depressed with her "spoiled identity." She can go forward, no longer clinging to the past and trying to recapture a time when it seemed her identity was intact. She instead moves ahead with a new self-confidence, with pride in her growing feeling of autonomy, and with respect for her feelings and needs, including the need for other people. Her new self can be involved in interdependencies without being defined by them. With this self-definition, she may be more able to live productively in the role of the formerly married woman, now single and alone. The transitional relationships with other widows have helped her to link her past self and her present self and to redefine her future self. In these relationships, she has received the knowledge of the changes she may need to make and has experienced one or more role models for how she may change.

The linking relationship by nature is temporary, and it changes as the widow changes from wife to widow to woman. As the new widow moves through the phases of transition, the help offered progresses from a focus on one-to-one assistance to help through involvement in a new community.

Impact

The bereaved wife almost invariably will cling to the past at first, denying the total change in her life situation. At this stage, the impact stage, her encounter with the widow aide is a potent tonic. The aide was once in the same situation and not only has survived but also has the vigor to reach out and help others. At the least, the new widow becomes aware that she is not totally isolated in her experience and so she feels less alone. At best, she sees grounds for hope that she, too, will survive. Her numbness and denial begin to recede as she becomes able to identify with a successful survivor. Although she still may feel distressed in a role that she never sought—that of bereaved wife—she begins to see alternatives. Personal contacts with another widow help her to acclimate to the reality of her husband's death and to acknowledge that the designation "widow" applies to her. Most widows at this stage are not ready to move out and join in group activities of any sort, but they appreciate the opportunity to talk and to listen:

> She never told me I should do this or that. She was there listening. You have to have someone you can tell your problems to.

Recoil

The widow's feelings begin to awaken during the second phase of transition, recoil, and she begins to acknowledge them openly and to accept them. Most widows do not feel it necessary to go over their feelings again and again. Some women need only to get them out once, while others need some review and more time. Since it helps at this stage to be reassured by other widows that these feelings are natural and legitimate, help often moves beyond the one-to-one meetings with the aide. Many widows are ready to join in a group discussion or an informal get-together where they learn from seeing other widows and from hearing their stories. Through the gatherings, the new widow also expands the audience for her own story, and she gains further confidence that her feelings are appropriate, that they are not pathological symptoms to be feared or depreciated. She becomes more realistic about who and where she is in her life:

> It may take as long as three years to realize that you really are a widow. Something snaps and all of a sudden you realize that you no longer have a husband to care for.

No longer denying or repressing their anguish, widows at this stage benefit from acknowledging their widowhood in a milieu of concerned and caring peers. As they develop an alliance with another widow or a group of widows, they can express the full range of their pain and anguish and can recognize fully that their lives will never be the same. The widows who have gone before show the newer widows other directions. They are role models and friends who can share their experience, and they guide the others in learning new skills. As a result, the new widow may consider going to school or work. She also senses a solidarity with other widows, begins to "re-people" her world, and focuses on activities. The need to talk over her widowhood and her feelings may recede at this time:

> We talked a lot. I needed to do that. But now too much talking about grief and death does no good. What is important is being active, going on trips, doing things together.

Accommodation

In making an accommodation, the widow typically develops a network of caring and understanding friends who support each other in moving on. She may be quite conscious of an identity shift as she develops new competencies for living as a single woman. At the same time that she is remembering the past with some pain and allowing herself to be sad, she feels some promise for her future. With accommodation she no longer feels isolated. She now has learned the new skills for building an appropriate new life, and she also has understanding friends with whom she can test her skills. In this type of exchange, widows practice with each other how to overcome their past socialization patterns and they learn with each other to value themselves as independent individuals. New identities develop as they practice and apply their new awareness and skills.

To accommodate fully, the widow must forge links between the past, the present, and the future. She no longer feels that her loss has made her a person who has no role to play. Her confidence in her ability to control her present and future life grows, and she sometimes may not recognize herself as the person she was in the past. Nonetheless, for her growth to take hold, the widow must recognize that her marriage has had a permanent impact on her life. She must accept and integrate her past; she will not forget it, act as if it never happened, or idealize it. She will honor the past but not live in it, perhaps by creating a memorial to her husband or perpetuating some tradition they once shared. But above all, she values herself for who she is in the here and now—a person with a background, heading into the future.

A few women did not find that talking was a useful means for them to move toward accommodation. These women did not suggest that they had no feelings, and they actively appreciated both the aide's involvement and the linkages to other widows. Eventually they, too, developed new and full lives, but they were not reflective about it:

> I'm very matter-of-fact. You have to learn to accept it. If I can't do anything about it, I just shut it off. I pull my shade down and I accept it. That's the story of my life.

Their coping strategies seemed as effective for them as did the styles of those women who chose to talk and reflect. One woman explained very simply that in the end it was up to her to deal with her own loneliness. We need to learn more about the approach of these women.

Some onlookers see remarriage as the solution to the widow's aloneness, but many women choose to remain unmarried:

> I might remarry someday, but it would have to be a very special man who could capture my interest. I couldn't go back to Mrs. Housewife again.

Other women remain unmarried because they have no option. Statistics being what they are, the choice of marriage is not available to most women who have been widowed. Accepting this is one of the challenges of accommodation:

> There is no substitute for the intimate sharing of marriage. It takes an "act of will" for us to accept this reality. You can do many things, but the fulfillment is only for you now, and there won't be anyone waiting at home to talk about it, as there once was.

The need to share remains even as a woman becomes more self-directed and independent. She has to learn to find alternate relationships that provide her with these opportunities. Although the intimacy associated with marriage may not be possible, other kinds of relationships can contribute a sense of completeness and wholeness to her life and can complement her newly found competence with a sense of mutuality. When a widow does remarry, she usually does not regress to her former self. She builds a new type of intimacy based on greater mutuality and interdependence. She usually does not remarry out of the fear of being alone but because she wants to share her life with someone. She goes into a relationship; she does not run from her life situation.

Accommodation ultimately means discovering that one's identity exists independently of the lost relationship and other relationships. The widow learns to form new relationships that both include mutualism and respect her competence and individuality. In the Widow-to-Widow project, this learning came largely from the linking relationships with other widows. During the accommodation stage, widows learn and practice developing relationships that do not require them to submerge their identities in others, and in which their achievement of autonomy is prized.

The Transition Ending: Completing a Cycle

At some point in the accommodation stage, the widow is ready to change her relationship to the mutual-help organization. Many women no longer feel the need to be involved and turn their attention to other activities, interests, and people. Others have continuing and strong associations that form the nucleus of their social lives. Still others become invested in the organization itself and devote a good deal of their time to its maintenance, thus completing the cycle of mutualism.

The cycle is complete when the now-experienced widow is ready to reach out and serve people who are newly arrived in the state of bereavement. The vitality of the mutual-help organization depends on generating new helpers, and helping others is yet another way for a widow to develop links between the future and the past and to maintain meaningful and caring relationships. With "a little help from some friends," the new widow can move her life in directions that would never have appeared had she not been widowed. Opportunity is created out of her unwanted crisis. Help takes the form of individual counseling that more closely resembles what a sensitive friend would offer than the help of a professionally trained helper. Over time the widow becomes involved in group activities and discussions with other widows and then becomes a helper in turn.

I cannot enumerate all the characteristics of those who decide to become helpers, but I know some of the characteristics of those who choose not to help and the motivators for those who do. Some widows cannot hear other people's problems without getting upset or becoming depressed. Others have made their peace with the past and choose not to review it. Those who become helpers must be willing to share their own pain and memories and to find some value for themselves in reaching out and talking with other widows:

> Helping others helped me. I learned about the problems of others. When people come to me, I can relate it to my own experience.

> My salvation is to give. You forget yourself . . . in giving . . . ; hearing others, you learn to know yourself better.

As long as the helper is gaining, too, she will find it worthwhile to remain in the helping role, though helping does not have the rewards of a job. When an aide is no longer learning, she may be ready to move on to other activities, making room for the next generation of helpers. Thus, mutual help as we applied it in the Widow-to-Widow program is well named. At any moment and over the long run, mutualism is the essence of the experience.

Epilogue

Nearly a dozen years have elapsed since we officially concluded the pilot Widow-to-Widow project at Harvard. Since then, much has happened in the field of bereavement.

The Widow-to-Widow program model has been replicated and adapted many times over, throughout the United States, Canada, and Western Europe. In the largest-scale effort, the American Association of Retired Persons (AARP) in 1974 began the Widowed Persons' Service. We consulted with AARP as they recruited and trained widowed people to organize chapters and to develop outreach, telephone service lines, and social activities. Today there are more than 135 local AARP programs for widowed people, and the Widowed Persons' Service publishes a directory and acts as a resource for an extensive network of widowed people's groups throughout the United States and Canada.[1]

Canadian groups such as Community Contact for the Widowed of Toronto were also modeled after the original Widow-to-Widow program. Countless local groups, too numerous to mention and too far-flung to identify, have followed the model and flourished. For example, To Live Again, which started in Philadelphia and has chapters across eastern Pennsylvania, has

---

[1]For information, write to Widowed Persons' Service, 1909 K Street N.W., Washington, DC.

over 1,000 members and recently celebrated its tenth anniversary.[2]

Other mutual-help groups that have sprung up or grown larger over the years employ a program design that differs somewhat from the Widow-to-Widow model in that they generally do not provide one-to-one outreach. Among these groups is THEOS (They Help Each Other Spiritually), which was started by Bea Decker in Pittsburgh and is now a national organization. Another is the Naim Conference, which began by serving the Archdiocese of Chicago in the early 1960s and now has branches in other midwestern cities. There are some groups that use the name "widow-to-widow" but provide either discussion groups led by a professional or are primarily social. Funeral directors across the country also have started projects or stimulated others to develop mutual-help efforts for the widowed. Today it is accepted practice for funeral services to sponsor or collaborate with widowed programs and other mutual-help efforts for bereaved people. Other bereavement-related groups have formed both to help individuals and to take social action on specific extraordinary circumstances of death. Mothers Against Drunk Driving is an example of the many groups of this type.

Still other interventions and organizations for bereaved people have arisen through professional or quasi-professional initiatives. The hospice movement, by 1983, had spawned 1,200 hospice programs in the United States alone. Though most hospice programs offer some services for the bereaved and sometimes bear the name "widow-to-widow," these services are generally not mutual-help programs but are run by bereavement counselors employed by the hospice. The 1976 Community Mental Health Act mandated that mental health centers, supported by federal funds, develop widowed-to-widowed programs as part of their preventive consultation and education efforts. Many professional people have been organizing and leading support groups. None of these efforts should be called mutual-help or Widow-to-Widow programs.

[2]Published materials to aid in replication of the Widow-to-Widow model include Silverman et al. (1974) and Silverman (1978, 1980).

Amid these developments, there was a growing interest in the efficacy of therapeutic interventions generally and in the field of death and dying particularly, and this generated a few studies of the various interventions (Parkes, 1980, 1981; Raphael, 1977). Still, the question of efficacy is unanswered, whether it is addressed to pure models of the Widow-to-Widow program versus other mutual-help variations, or to mutual help versus psychotherapy or other professional help.

Only one controled study, conducted in Toronto, Canada, has examined a program closely approximating the Widow-to-Widow program (Vachon et al., 1980). Vachon and her colleagues (1982) found that people receiving the service adapted better and more rapidly than those in a control group. Also, among people who were rated as having a high risk for emotional illness at the outset, those who received services were more likely to move to low-risk status than were members of the control group.

Videka-Sherman and Lieberman (1985) studied the impact of mutual help versus professional help in Chicago. In their extensive study of the Compassionate Friends they found that the mutual-help experience led to greater positive change than professional help.

Lieberman and Borman (1981) compared the members of 71 THEOS groups in the United States and Canada with widowed people who had decided not to join. They found that the more intense a person's involvement with the group, the better the outcome with regard to self-esteem and absence of depressive symptoms.

Even though conclusions cannot be drawn from so few and such small studies, the professional literature on the value of mutual help continues to grow (Gartner & Reisman, 1984; Gottlieb, 1984). Some materials offer specific direction for how professional people can work with these groups (Gartner & Reisman, 1980; Silverman, 1980).

This trend received further stimulation from the recent state-of-the-art study by the Institute of Medicine of the National Academy of Science (Osterweis, 1984). Although it was found that variations in the interventions prevented making any conclusions about the relative effectiveness of mutual-support groups, hospices, or psychotherapy, the researchers affirmed the value of intervening. Everyone, they pointed out, needs some help following bereavement. For many people, effective help will come most appropriately and naturally from family, friends, and existing social-support networks. Indeed, adequate social support is a documented prerequisite to successful adaptation. For the few bereaved people who have serious preexisting physical or mental vulnerabilities, professional assistance may be mandatory, if only for assessment.

In between the two poles—intervention for people with predisposing illness and nonintervention for people with rich and effective social-support networks—we are still left with using our best judgment regarding the preferred social response to large numbers of bereaved people. For many people, mutual-help or some other intervention could make the difference between a slow, agonizing process and a relatively smooth, less prolonged adaptation. Not surprisingly, my own judgment is that the Widow-to-Widow model has advantages here, both over professionally led assistance and over the less comprehensive mutual-help models.

Mutual help generally has an advantage over professional help since it does not treat a person as ill and has an image-enhancing emphasis on learning from peers. I believe that the Widow-to-Widow model has advantages over other mutual-help models since it offers a range of entry points. No one reached has to accept, but everyone in need has more than one opportunity to accept. A person can refuse the offer of help at one point and enter at another. Some people who respond to one-to-one outreach may never join a group. Others who would not respond to outreach may later join a group. Still others may find it helpful only to talk with someone on the telephone. Though I cannot actually say that these principles of program design make a difference in patterns of service use or ultimate outcome, the data do show that many widows appreciated the program's sensitivity to their individual styles. Such a sensitivity, reflected in program design and in respect for program participants, should be a hallmark of any human service.

In the end I am not only talking about a particular program or service but a way of helping people to create more caring communities. It has been the essence of this work that through mutual help an environment is created that minimizes barriers between people. This type of environment legitimates people's need for each other and their ability to use their experience on each other's behalf:

> If I can ease one person's pain by sharing mine, then mine will have not been in vain. In helping others I help myself as well.

References

Abrahams, R. B. (1972). Mutual help for the widowed. *Social Work*, *17*, 55-61.

Abrahams, R. B. (1976). Mutual helping: Styles of caregiving in a mutual aid program—The Widowed Service Line. In G. Caplan and M. Killilea (Eds.), *Support systems and mutual help*. New York: Grune and Stratton.

Agee, J. (1957). *A death in the family*. New York: McDowell, Obolensky.

Anderson, R. (1974). Notes of a survivor. In S. B. Troup and W. A. Greene (Eds.), *The patient, death, and the family*. New York: Scribners.

Arling, G. (1976). The elderly widow and her family, neighbors and friends. *Journal of Marriage and the Family*, *3*(4), 757-768.

Bandura, A. (1977). *Social learning theory*. Englewood Cliffs, NJ: Prentice-Hall.

Barrett, C. J. (1977). Effectiveness of widows' groups in facilitating change. *Journal of Consulting and Clinical Psychology*, *46*(1), 20-31.

Bowlby, J. (1961). Processes of mourning. *International Journal of Psychoanalysis*, *44*, 317.

Bowlby, J. (1969-1980). *Attachment and loss* (Vols. 1-3). New York: Basic Books.

Broverman, I. K., Vogel, S., Broverman, D., Clarkson, F., and Rosenkrantz, P. (1970). Sex role stereotypes and clinical judgments of mental health. *Journal of Consulting and Clinical Psychology*, *3*(February), 1-7.

Deutsch, H. (1945). *The psychology of women: A psychoanalytic interpretation* (Vol. 2). New York: Grune and Stratton.

213

Engel, G. L. (1961). Is grief a disease? *Psychosomatic Medicine, 23,* 18–22.

Feldman, R. (1979). *The ambition of ghosts.* New York: Green River Press.

Freeman, J. (1973). Woman and the American scene. In C. R. Stimpson (Ed.), *Discrimination against women: Congressional hearings on equal rights in education and employment.* New York: R. R. Bowker.

Friedan, B. (1964). *The feminine mystique.* New York: Dell.

Friedan, B. (1976). *It changed my life.* New York: Random House.

Friedson, E. (1970). Dominant professions, bureaucracy, and client services. In W. Rosengren and M. Lefton (Eds.), *Organizations and clients.* Columbus, OH: Merrill.

Gartner, A., and Reisman, F. (1980). *Help: A working guide to self help groups.* New York: New Viewpoints, Viscom Press.

Gartner, A., and Reisman, F. (1984). *The self help revolution.* New York: Human Sciences Press.

Gilligan, C. (1982). *In a different voice.* Cambridge, MA: Harvard University Press.

Goffman, E. (1963). *Stigma: Notes on the management of spoiled identities.* Englewood Cliffs, NJ: Prentice-Hall.

Golan, N. (1975). Wife to Widow to Woman. *Social Work, 20,* 369–374.

Gorer, G. (1965). *Death, grief and mourning.* Garden City, NY: Doubleday.

Gottlieb, B. (1984). *Social support strategies.* Beverly Hills, CA: Sage.

Gurin, G., Veroff, J., and Feld, S. (1960). *Americans View Their Mental Health.* New York: Basic Books.

Hamburg, D. A., and Adams, J. E. (1967). A perspective on coping: Seeking and utilizing information in major transitions. *Archives of General Psychiatry, 17:* 277–284.

Howell, E. (1981). Women: From Freud to the present. In E. Howell and M. Bayes (Eds.), *Women and mental health.* New York: Basic Books.

Kegan, R. (1982). *The evolving self.* Cambridge, MA: Harvard University Press.

Kohlberg, L. (1969). Stage and sequence: The cognitive developmental approach to socialization. In D. Goslin (Ed.), *Handbook of Socialization: Theory and Research.* New York: Rand McNally.

Kropotkin, P. (1902; reprinted 1972). *Mutual Aid.* New York: University Press.

Kübler-Ross, E. (1969). *On death and dying.* New York: Macmillan.

Lazare, A. (1979). Unresolved grief. In A. Lazare (Ed.), *Out-patient psychiatry: Diagnosis and treatment.* Baltimore: Williams and Wilkins.

Lenneberg, E. (1970). Mutual aid. In E. Lenneberg and J. L. Rowbotham (Eds.), *The illeostomy patient.* Springfield, IL: Charles C Thomas.

Levine, M., and Levine, A. (1970). *A social history of helping services.* Boston: Appleton-Century-Crofts.

Levinson, D. J., Darrow, C. N., Klein, E. B., Levinson, M. H., and McKee, B. (1978). *Seasons of a man's life.* New York: Ballantine Books.

Lieberman, M., and Borman, L. (Eds.). (1979). *Self help groups for coping with crisis.* San Francisco: Jossey-Bass.

Lieberman, M., and Borman, L. (1981). Researchers study THEOS: Report groups effect big help to members. *THEOS, 20,* 3-6.

Lifton, R. J. (1973). Home from the war. New York: Simon and Schuster.

Lifton, R. J. (1974). Symbolic immortality. In S. B. Troup and W. A. Greene (Eds.), *The patient, death, and the family.* New York: Scribners.

Lifton, R. J. (1979). *The broken connection.* New York: Simon and Schuster.

Lindemann, E. (1944). The symptomatology and management of acute grief. *American Journal of Psychiatry, 101,* 141.

Loevinger, J. (1980). *Ego development: Conceptions and theories.* San Francisco: Jossey-Bass.

Lopata, H. (1973). *Widowhood in an American city.* Cambridge, MA: Schenkman.

Lopata, H. (1979). *Women as widows: Support systems.* New York: Elsevier.

Maddison, D., and Raphael, B. (1976). Death of a spouse. In H. Grunebaum and J. Crist (Eds.), *Contemporary marriage: Structure, dynamics and therapy.* Boston: Little, Brown.

Maddison, D., and Walker, W. L. (1967). Factors affecting the outcome of conjugal bereavement. *British Journal of Psychiatry, 113,* 1057-1067.

Mahler, M. (1968). *On human symbiosis and the vicissitudes of individuation.* New York: International Universities Press.

Marris, P. (1958). *Widows and their families.* London: Routledge and Kegan Paul.

Marris, P. (1974). *Loss and change.* New York: Pantheon.

Maslow, A. H. (1970). *Motivation and personality.* New York: Harper & Row.

Meyers, J. (1976). Introduction. In P. R. Silverman (Ed.), *If you will lift the load, I will lift it too.* New York: Jewish Funeral Directors.

Meyers, J. E., and Timms, N. (1969). Clash in perspective between worker and client. *Social Casework, 50,* 32–40.

Miller, J. B. (1976). *The new psychology of women.* Boston: Beacon Press.

Osterweis, M., Solomon, F., and Green, M. (1984). *Bereavement: Reactions, consequences and care.* Washington, DC: National Academy Press.

Parkes, C. M. (1972). *Bereavement.* New York: International Universities Press.

Parkes, C. M. (1977). Bereavement and mental illness. Part 1: A clinical study of the grief of bereaved psychiatric patients. Part 2: A classification of bereavement reactions. *British Journal of Medical Psychology, 38,* 1.

Parkes, C. M. (1980). Bereavement counselling: Does it work? *British Medical Journal, 281,* 3–6.

Parkes, C. M. (1981). Evaluation of a bereavement service. *Journal of Preventive Psychiatry, 1,* 179–188.

Piaget, J. (1965). *The moral judgement of the child.* New York: Free Press.

Pincus, L. (1975). *Death and the family.* New York: Random House.

Raphael, B. (1977). Preventive intervention with the recently bereaved. *Archives of General Psychiatry, 34,* 1450–1454.

Rothman, S. M. (1978). *Women's proper place.* New York: Basic Books.

Rubin, Z. (1980). *Children's friendships.* Cambridge, MA: Harvard University Press.

Scarf, M. (1980). *Unfinished business: Pressure points in the lives of women.* New York: Doubleday.

Schacter, S. (1959). *The psychology of affiliation.* Stanford, CA: Stanford Press.

Seskin, J. (1975). *Young Widow.* New York: Ace Books.

Sheehy, G. (1976). *Passages.* New York: E. P. Dutton.

Silver, R. L., and Wortman, C. B. (1980). Coping with undesirable life events. In J. Garber and M. L. Seligman (Eds.), *Human helplessness.* New York: Academic Press.

Silverman, P. R. (1966). Services for the widowed during the period of bereavement. *Social Work Practice*. New York: Columbia University Press.

Silverman, P. R. (1967). Services to the widowed: First steps in a program of preventive intervention. *Community Mental Health Journal, 3*, 37–44.

Silverman, P. R. (1969a). Clients who drop out: A study of spoiled helping relationships. Unpublished Ph.D. Dissertation, Florence Heller School, Brandeis University.

Silverman, P. R. (1969b). The Widow-to-Widow program: An experiment in preventive intervention. *Mental Hygiene, 53*, 333–337.

Silverman, P. R. (1970). The widow as a caregiver in a program of preventive intervention with other widows. *Mental Hygiene, 54*, 540–547.

Silverman, P. R. (1972). Widowhood and preventive intervention. *The Family Coordinator, 21*,1, 95–102.

Silverman, P. R. (1977). *If you will lift the load: A guide to the creation of widowed-to-widowed services*. New York: Jewish Funeral Directors of America.

Silverman, P. R. (1978). *Mutual help: A guide for mental health workers* (NIMH, DHEW Publication No. ADM 78-646). Washington, DC: U.S. Government Printing Office.

Silverman, P. R. (1980). *Mutual help groups: Organization and development*. Beverly Hills, CA: Sage.

Silverman, P. R. (1981). *Helping women cope with grief*. Beverly Hills, CA: Sage.

Silverman, P. R., and Cooperband, A. (1975). Mutual help and the elderly widow. *Journal of Geriatric Psychiatry, 8*, 9–27.

Silverman, P. R., MacKenzie, D., Pettipas, M., and Wilson, E. W. (Eds.). (1974). *Helping each other in widowhood*. New York: Health Sciences.

Silverman, P. R., and Smith, D. (1984). "Helping" in mutual help groups for the physically disabled. In F. Gartner and F. Reisman (Eds.), *The Self-Help Revolution*. New York: Human Sciences Press.

Silverman, S. M., and Silverman, P. R. (1979). Parent–child communication in widowed families. *American Journal of Psychotherapy, 33*, 428–441.

Sullivan, H. S. (1953). *The interpersonal theory of psychiatry*. New York: W. W. Norton.

Tavris, C., and Offir, C. (1977). *The longest war: Sex differences in perspective*. New York: Harcourt, Brace and Jovanovich.

Tyhurst, J. (1958). The role of transition states—Including disasters in mental illness. In *Symposium on Preventive and Social Psychiatry*. Washington, DC: U.S. Government Printing Office.

Vachon, M. L. S., Sheldon, A. R., Lancie, W. J., Lyall, W. A. L., Rogers, J., and Freeman, S. J. (1980). A controlled study of self-help interventions for widows. *American Journal of Psychiatry, 137*, 1380–1384.

Vachon, M. L. S. (1982). Grief and bereavement: The family's experience before and after death. In I. Gentles (Ed.), *Care for the dying and the bereaved*. Toronto: Anglican Book Centre.

Van Gennup, A. (1960). *The rites of passage*. Chicago: University of Chicago Press.

Videka-Sherman, L., and Lieberman, M. (1985). The effects of self-help and psychotherapy intervention on child loss: The limits of recovery. *American Journal of Orthopsychiatry, 55*, 1, 70–72.

Von Witzleben, H. D. (1958). On loneliness. *Psychiatry, 21*, 37–43.

Weiss, R. S. (1969). The fund of sociability. *Transaction, 6*(9), 36–43.

Weissman, A. (1977). *On death and denying*. New York: Behavioral Publications.

White, R. W. (1974). Strategies of adaptation: An attempt at systematic description. In G. V. Coelho, et al. (Eds.), *Coping and adaptation*. New York: Basic Books.

Index

Index